WILL
GARBUTT

WILLIAM GARBUTT

The Father of Italian Football

Paul Edgerton

SPORTS
BOOKS

Published by SportsBooks Ltd

Copyright: Paul Edgerton©
October 2009

SportsBooks Limited
PO Box 422
Cheltenham
GL50 2YN
United Kingdom
Tel: 01242 256755
Fax: 0560 3108126
email   randall@sportsbooks.ltd.uk
Website   www.sportsbooks.ltd.uk

Cover designed by Alan Hunns.

A CIP catalogue record for this book is available from the British Library.

ISBN 9781899807 82 6

Printed in the UK by Cromwell Press Group

*Dedicated to my son Tom and
to the memory of my Mother*

Contents

Introduction

During the World Cup held in Spain in 1982, I felt at odds with the rest of Britain. While the media and public were purring with delight at the performances of Brazil, who boasted the creative talents of players like Zico, Falcao and Socrates among their number, it was the defending of the Italians, whether the effortless elegance of Gaetano Scirea or the brutal efficiency of the assassin Claudio Gentile, that caught my eye.

Since then I have been something of an Italophile and as such thought I knew a thing or two about the Italian game. However, the contribution made to *calcio* during the first half of the twentieth century by an Englishman named William Thomas Garbutt had completely eluded me until I read John Foot's *Calcio, History of Italian Football* while on holiday in 2006. Foot's brief snippet of information intrigued me and on my return I began investigating the man's career as a player and manager.

As far as I was aware, the British professional footballer had invariably struggled to settle overseas.

Denis Law was hailed by United's Stretford End as the king but had endured a miserable time with Torino, and Jimmy Greaves became so disillusioned with life in Milan that he is reported to have fled back to England in his own car in the dead of night. Ian Rush seemed to score goals with ease in a Liverpool shirt but found the going much tougher with Juventus and famously complained that pasta was giving him headaches.

So, it was a pleasant surprise to hear of a Briton who had settled in a foreign land and been a resounding success, and as long ago as 1912 at that. Aged only twenty-nine, and with his playing career only just behind him, Garbutt uprooted his young family from their native Lancashire, and set off for the port of Genova in Italy to bring professionalism to the infant Italian game. It did not take long for his efforts to bear fruit, Genoa winning the Italian championship on three occasions under his leadership.

He worked closely with Vittorio Pozzo, the man who would go on to lead Italy to victory in the 1934 and 1938 World Cups, along with the gold medal for the 1936 Olympic football tournament. The success Garbutt brought to Genoa was eyed enviously by other leading clubs such as Internazionale, Juventus and Bologna, and the rapid improvement in the standard of the domestic game was in direct relation to its success on the global stage.

Regrettably, the insular world of British professional football largely ignored Garbutt's work, not only in Italy, but also in Spain, where he coached Athletic Bilbao to the championship.

Introduction

In the early stages of researching Garbutt's life I visited his final home in Priory Road, Warwick, with my son Tom. The tiny terraced house seemed a small return for his immense contribution to the game and Tom and I began to contrast this with the wealth enjoyed by today's modern football professionals, both players and managers alike. I thought out aloud that it seemed 'a poor return for a …' but was unable to find a fitting description.

Filling the void, Tom suggested, 'legend?'

And you know, despite the fact that the vast majority of his countrymen have never heard of his name, let alone are aware of his achievements, I think the tribute is apt.

There are a number of people I would like to thank for their kindness and generosity during the writing of this book. Thank you to Steve Cook, Spencer McKenna and Phil Harvey for proof-reading and critical feedback, to Jane Barcoe for access to private family correspondence and to Ron Furnace for providing me with a photograph of his father and the young Garbutt, team members of the local junior side. Thanks also to William's nephew, Eric Garbutt, for information relating to the wider Garbutt family tree.

My gratitude also to Martin Clifford and Danielle Coghill for their professional advice and to the writers and sports historians Davide Rota and Aldo Padovano for their invaluable assistance.

My thanks and love is due to Tom and Jennie, for all the encouragement and support they have given me, and for putting up with my regular absences, both physical and emotional, during the course of writing this book.

Last but by no means least, my deep gratitude and affection go to Bill and Maria Welsh, not only for the information, access to Garbutt family letters and photographs, but also for the wonderful hospitality they gave me during our frequent conversations. Sadly Maria died two months before this book was published.

Paul Edgerton February 2009

Chapter 1

The End of a Career

The prolonged heatwave endured by most of the country in 1911 had recently ended and the flat-capped followers of Blackburn Rovers stood crammed on the terraces of Ewood Park under more familiar cloudy skies.

Four matches into the new season, on 16 September, the home game against Notts County was William Garbutt's first. Until recently his name would have been among the first written down on the Blackburn team sheet but the signing of a new outside right for a record transfer fee had seen him lose his place in the side. A good performance today would give his manager something to think about, and could see him force his way back. As usual, he patrolled the touchline, waiting patiently for the ball to find him, where time and again he would display the art of the winger, hoping to tease the full back, jinking this way and that, before launching the heavy leather football into the penalty area in a graceful arc, where it would land perfectly time and again for the advancing centre forward to head home.

Once more, the ball came out to Garbutt, his team-mates searching for him as their creative outlet. The gathered throng craned their necks for a better view.

On this last occasion however, he failed to get the better of the full back. Brute force, this time, had beaten artistry. A sickening clash of skin, bone and leather and Garbutt writhed in agony in a heap on the ground. The sport of association football had little room for sentiment; the game continued as Garbutt lay receiving attention on the touchline, men and boys in the crowd offering the odd shout of encouragement. Raising himself against the trainer, Garbutt climbed slowly to his feet and attempted to cajole his battered and bruised body into action. It was all in vain. A searing pain shot through the length of his leg. He knew in his heart of hearts that the game was up for him for today at least. And as for the future, who could tell?

William Thomas Garbutt was born 9 January 1883 at the family home in London Road, Hazel Grove, Stockport. Whether his parents Thomas and Emily were desperate for a boy can only be summised, but they certainly displayed determination. Before William came Jane Elizabeth, Ada Margaret, Annie Gleave, Margaret Emily, Florence Rebecca, Nellie and Kate. Large families were the rule rather than the exception.[1]

Few families escaped the spectre of the death of a child at this time however, and the Garbutts were no exception. Ada Margaret, Thomas and Emily's second child, had died before her second year and an older brother, Joseph Skeen Garbutt, had also died, aged only two and a half, a mere eleven days after William's arrival. Poor sanitary conditions, nutrition and health care, overcrowding, all of these factors contributed to a high infant mortality rate.[2] Following the birth of another son, Charles, in 1888, the Garbutt clan was at last complete and William shared the crowded family home with his parents, maternal grandmother, six sisters and a brother. William's father, Thomas Skeen Garbutt, was a master joiner. Despite having a trade, work was in short supply and the large family struggled to make ends meet.

A report for the Manchester Statistical Society in 1889 revealed that more than forty per cent of working men interviewed in nearby Salford were 'irregularly employed' and more than sixty per cent could be defined as 'very poor', that is with a weekly income of less than four shillings per week.[3] Neither could Stockport be described as a pleasant place to live at the time. Following his tour of working-class England, Frederick Engels reported somewhat snootily:

> *Stockport is notoriously one of the darkest and smokiest holes in the whole industrial area, and particularly when seen from the viaduct, presents a truly revolting picture. But the cottages and cellar dwellings of the workers are even more unpleasant to look at. They stretch in long rows through all parts of the town from the bottom of the valley*

to the crests of the hills. I do not remember seeing elsewhere in the Manchester industrial district as many inhabited cellars in proportion to the number of homes.[4]

Although Engels wrote these words more than forty years before Garbutt's birth, conditions had hardly improved.

Hazel Grove had originally been known as Bullock Smithy after one Richard Bullock had leased land from John Turkington in 1560 to establish a smithy, which stood at the junction of several roads including the main Stockport to Macclesfield roads. Perhaps not surprisingly, the name Bullock Smithy attracted negative attention and the locals became the butt of jokes. The *Manchester Guardian* carried a story of an auctioneer who was in the process of selling a rare book. Failing dismally to attract any interest he enquired of his audience: 'Come on, where's tha' al from? Bullock Smithy? Because tha' don't know a book from a brick.'

In 1750, the Methodist John Wesley described it as 'one of the most famous villages in the country for all manner of wickedness', most likely referring to the locals' appetite for a variety of vices ranging from gambling to cock, bull and dog fighting. Understandably, locals came to resent the name and on 26 September 1836 the village voted to officially change to the more genteel sounding Hazel Grove.

Tragedy struck the family again when Thomas Skeen Garbutt died aged fifty-one and was buried in the churchyard at Norbury Church, Hazel Grove,

Stockport on 23 September 1891. The family gathered around the mound of freshly dug earth, and, mindful of the grief of his sisters and mother, William stifled his own tears. He was just eight years old.

Despite the undoubted hardship, the Garbutts displayed strong, traditional family values. The children were clean, well groomed and as well nourished as the available money would allow. Educational attainment was considered important, and two of William's sisters, Annie and Florence, were schoolmistresses. This was a cause of great pride to the family, particularly to their mother Emily.

Although William was a bright, intelligent child, he did not share his sisters' penchant for spending time pondering books. His devotion to football was evident from an early age and he would spend every possible waking moment playing with friends or kicking the ball alone, against one of the omnipresent brick walls in his neighbourhood. It was here on the streets of Stockport that he honed the skills that would turn him into a professional at the highest levels of the English game and enable him, in time, to pass these skills on to two European nations that would become footballing super powers and where the game would become a quasi-religious event. All this was years into the future, however.

Perhaps the earliest known photograph of William shows him as a fresh-faced youngster (maybe thirteen or so) sitting cross legged, arms folded, as a member of Edgeley Football Club. His head slightly tilted to one side, he seems lost in his thoughts, perhaps dreaming of playing one day on a much larger stage.

William seems to have inherited his father's practical abilities for upon finishing his education he found employment locally as a box maker. His weekly wage, though meagre, was nevertheless crucial in helping his mother to make ends meet, and William, as the senior male in the family, was proud of the contribution that he was able to make. Life as a box maker would not do for him in the long term, however. He needed to break free from the Stockport streets and see some of the world.

Although he cared deeply for his family, the love provided by a mother and six sisters could be suffocating. And so, as has many a young man from working-class backgrounds from that day to this, Garbutt joined the Royal Artillery. By 1902, at the age of nineteen, William was serving his country in Clonnel, Ireland.

Shortly after joining up, he was summoned to a superior. Marching in and saluting the officer before him, he was invited to sit down. The officer fidgeted and averted his gaze, but eventually William was informed that his mother, Emily Elizabeth Garbutt, had died. Now without either parent and not yet twenty years old, William needed to grow up quickly.

Despite being a professional soldier, William's mastery of a football was evident and he became an obvious choice for the Royal Artillery football team. Regimental prestige was important, and Garbutt's seniors saw in him an effective weapon to be used against opponents. It was while playing in these regimental games that Garbutt was spotted by officials of Reading FC, then playing in the Southern League. Whether or not Garbutt signed on a full-time basis for Reading is uncertain but an article in *Athletic News*, a popular weekly sports newspaper of the time, heralded his arrival at Reading thus:

Garbutt (99th Battery RFA) did himself well in several army competitions and on a few occasions figured in the Reading ranks with considerable success.[5]

What we do know is that he made just one appearance in the dark blue and white stripes of Reading in the 1904–05 season, making a further seven in the next campaign and registering a solitary goal.

A player of Garbutt's ability was not going to be playing in the Southern League for long, however, and scouts for Woolwich Arsenal recommended him to the London club. Under the heading 'Transfer of Garbutt' *Athletic News* reported on his move south to the London club:

Reading's dashing outside right W. Garbutt was on Saturday transferred to Woolwich Arsenal. The transfer was effected with much regret by the Reading board of directors, who, after fully considering the matter, felt compelled to act in such a manner. A goodly sum has been agreed upon and a full league team will visit Reading the first week of September 1906 as part of the business. Garbutt has rendered invaluable service to the club this season, and his

*departure will be much regretted. Garbutt had
made himself exceedingly popular with the Reading
crowd, and it is absolutely certain, bar accidents,
that the ex-soldier is destined to make a great name
for himself in the first league or any other football.
By the way, Garbutt is in his 22nd year, stands 5'
8', and turns the scale at just over 11st.*[6]

Prophetic words indeed. On 23 December 1905,
Garbutt, along with his new team-mates, returned
to his native north-west where he made his debut
in a 2-2 draw against Preston North End. He must
have thought how good it would have been had his
parents been in the crowd that day. In those days,
games came thick and fast and the team returned
south to London in readiness for their next fixture,
scheduled to take place on Christmas Day.

Garbutt played his part in making it a
memorable Christmas for the twenty thousand
home supporters in the Manor Ground, scoring
one goal in their 4-3 defeat of Newcastle United.
He was to make a total of nineteen appearances
in the league for Woolwich Arsenal that season
(scoring four goals) but it was his contribution
to a successful run in the FA Cup that would fire
the imagination of the club's supporters. Prior to
this, Garbutt's first season in the side, Woolwich
Arsenal had never ventured beyond the second
round in their twenty-year history.

Expectations among even the most loyal of their
followers were low when they began the campaign,
especially after they had been able only to draw at

home to West Ham United in early January 1906. They travelled the few short miles to contest the replay with West Ham five days later and went through to the second round after recording a fine 3-2 win in which Garbutt scored.

A home tie against Watford was next up and a comfortable 3-0 home win saw the Gunners through to the unknown territory of the third round. Again drawn at home, this time Sunderland would provide the opposition, in what was bound to be their toughest test to date. Remarkably, and in front of twenty-seven thousand delirious home supporters, the Wearsiders were brushed aside 5-0. Garbutt scored the only hat-trick of his professional career in this game and Woolwich Arsenal were through to the fourth round, where they would play away to Manchester United on 10 March 1906.

In front of twenty-six and a half thousand partisan Mancunians, Woolwich Arsenal swept to a 3-2 victory. Amazingly, they found themselves in the FA Cup semi-final. Standing in their way of a place in the final was the might of Newcastle United. The Geordies were to appear in five FA Cup finals between 1905 and 1911, winning just once. For all their efforts, Arsenal were to prove little match for Newcastle on the day, losing 2-0 in the game played at Stoke City's Victoria Ground on 31 March 1906.

Despite his ultimate disappointment, the tournament had been a personal triumph for Garbutt. He had played in each of the six games taken to reach the semi-final and ended up as the London side's top scorer with four goals.

Garbutt was again to ply his trade with Arsenal in the 1906–07 season, and, despite being plagued by a series of injuries, made twenty-five league appearances, finding the net on three occasions. It was his prowess as a supplier of crosses for Arsenal's forward triumvirate of Coleman, Kyle and Satterthwaite that was his most telling contribution to the side, however, with those three scoring fifteen, thirteen and seventeen goals respectively.

The side improved its league position from the season before (from twelfth to seventh) but it was another extended run in the FA Cup that was to prove the main talking point among the Arsenal faithful. Grimsby were their first opponents and Garbutt scored in both the 1-1 away draw and the 3-0 home win in the replay. There was something about the FA Cup that agreed with Garbutt. Both Bristol clubs (City then Rovers) were beaten in the second and third rounds. A victory against Barnsley would need to be gained if the Gunners were to repeat the previous season's feat of reaching the last four of the competition. This was duly achieved with a 2-1 win, after being a goal down at half-time.

Their opponents in the semi-final were to be another Yorkshire club, Sheffield Wednesday. Garbutt was part of the line-up that took to the field on 23 March 1907 at the newly opened St Andrew's stadium in Birmingham in front of thirty-six thousand supporters. When Garbutt headed home a cross by Satterthwaite to give Arsenal the lead, he must have allowed himself to dream that he was going to appear in football's showpiece occasion. Not for the last time, however, Garbutt was to see how a twist of fate, one single moment, can change the course, not only of a game, but also one's life. Jimmy Ashcroft, the Arsenal goalkeeper, was injured in a collision and forced to leave the field. Down to ten men in an era before substitutes, and without an experienced goalkeeper, the disruption to the Londoners proved to be crucial and before half-time, the score was levelled. Wednesday inflicted two further blows in the second half and ran out 3-1 winners. Garbutt's FA Cup dreams were dashed for the second successive season and he would need to wait a while longer for footballing glory to come his way.

He was to make only eight league appearances for Woolwich Arsenal in the 1907–08 season (scoring two goals), his penultimate game being an away tie against the league leaders Manchester United. The fact that United's Clayton pitch resembled a mud bath did not prevent players from both sides contesting the game at a high pace. The *Manchester Guardian* wrote that Garbutt, following 'one fine individual effort' levelled for the Gunners, before the home side triumphed. Although Arsenal lost 4-2, Garbutt was acclaimed as their best forward by the paper.

But on 5 May 1908, Garbutt was to leave Arsenal, heading back to the north-west to join Blackburn Rovers. Ironically, his last game for Woolwich Arsenal had been a home tie against Blackburn at the end of November 1907. The London side had amassed debts and Garbutt, along with a number of other saleable assets, was sold to reduce them.

At the age of twenty-five and at the peak of his playing career, his capital adventure was over. Lawrence Cotton, Blackburn Rovers' ambitious and wealthy chairman and local businessman, had been persuaded to stump up the cash for Garbutt. The Rovers had endured a disastrous season in 1907–08, not only finishing a dire fourteenth in the league but also being dumped out of the FA Cup in the first round by second division Leicester Fosse. It was obvious that fresh blood was required.

Garbutt's signing coincided with the appointment of a new trainer in the guise of Bob Holmes. Holmes was a no-nonsense ex-professional who had been an ever-present member of the Preston North End 'Invincibles' that had triumphed in the English football league's inaugural championship in 1888, and a founder member of the first footballers' trades union, the Association Footballers' Union. Garbutt learned a great deal from Holmes that he would put into good effect when he hung up his boots. It seems that Garbutt took a little time to settle into his new side if the comments of the football correspondent for the *Northern Daily Telegraph* are anything to go by. Following his debut for Rovers in front of the Ewood Park faithful, Quilp writes:

> *The star performer of the forward line was without question Kyle.* (Archie Kyle had been one of the first Catholics to play for Glasgow Rangers before signing for Blackburn). *He was the cleverest attacker on the field. There was nothing haphazard about his work. His passing and shooting alike being*

splendid. Anthony and he made by far the most effective wing. Ellis too at inside right worked with judgement but Garbutt and Davies were off colour.

And again in the contest between Rovers and Liverpool some eleven days later, 'Garbutt and Wombwell could hardly be recognised as the two men who played such pretty and effective football at Manchester.'

Hardly an auspicious start in his new surroundings, then. As the season progressed, however, and Garbutt and his team-mates began to adapt to Bob Holmes' fitness regime, both Garbutt's individual performances and the team's results began to improve, to such an extent that it is worth repeating at length Quilp's match report printed in the *Northern Daily Telegraph* for the 8-1 thrashing of Sunderland on 22 March 1909.

Headlined 'The brilliance of Garbutt', Quilp enthuses:

It is not a difficult matter to show how this crop of goals were scored. While giving every credit to the inside trio, Latheron, Ellis-Crompton and Aitkenhead for their goalscoring abilities, one cannot deny the fact that the star of the line was Garbutt. I mentioned in this column yesterday how he showed more vigorous play and cleverer tactics than usual at Manchester (referring to his part in a 3-0 away win at Manchester United two days earlier) *but that exhibition was poor if it be compared with Monday's against the Wearsiders.*

It was a display worthy of Meredith at his best, particularly with regard to his centering. Time after time he planted the ball right in front of the goal. Six times in all did Latheron (1), Crompton (3) and Aitkenhead (2) turn those middles to account and Garbutt obtained a goal himself. Therefore, he had a hand in seven goals, which I should say, is a record for any outside-right in a league match.

Furthermore, Garbutt had been the architect of a result 'so unexpected that it caused quite a sensation throughout the country'.[7]

All told, it was a productive campaign both for Blackburn Rovers and for Garbutt. His twenty-nine appearances and two goals contributed to Blackburn's fourth place finish in the league, an impressive climb of ten places on the previous season. Perhaps the zenith of Garbutt's career as a professional footballer came as a result of the 3-1 away win to Middlesbrough on 23 October 1909, a victory that took Blackburn Rovers to the top of the First Division.

In his own inimitable style, 'Quilp' enthused in the *Northern Daily Telegraph*

Let me take the first available opportunity of extending congratulations to the Blackburn Rovers players on having carried the club to the head of affairs in the First Division. It matters not if they only keep where they are for a week; they have accomplished a feat which has not been equalled in recent years, and one has only to compare the present record with that of twelve months ago at this time (when the club lay in eighth place) to show what an advance has been made.[8]

Williamson, the home goalkeeper, had performed heroically to ensure the home goal was not breached but Blackburn could not be denied for the entire match. 'Quilp' goes on:

He (Williamson) failed to negotiate properly a drive from Latheron, and the ball went from his hands to Garbutt who was standing to the right of the upright. The winger could not possibly have scored from where he was, but he dribbled back until he got into a favourable position, and then touched the ball into the net.

At the end of the game, the victorious Blackburn players and officials dashed away from the Middlesbrough ground to catch their train back to the north-west, remaining unaware that they had reached the summit of English football until they had to change trains at Leeds almost three hours later. Then, as 'Quilp' reports, 'their cup of joy was full to overflowing.'

Despite being unable to remain at the top of the league, Rovers still finished a creditable third. Their tally of forty-five points was a club record. Garbutt had once again made twenty-nine appearances, this time weighing in with three league goals.

Another high point of Garbutt's domestic playing career came on 26 February 1910, when he was selected for an English Football League XI to take on the Scottish Football League. His usual 'workplace' of Ewood Park had been selected to host the game and recent improvements to the stadium meant that a large crowd could be accommodated in relative comfort.

All of the players representing the English XI played for teams in the top half of the football league and all but two of them for northern sides. The game was played out in front of twenty thousand supporters who had refused to allow the snowy conditions to dampen their spirits.

Garbutt played an effective part in the game, with the *Northern Daily Telegraph* reporting:

It was particularly pleasing to the majority of the spectators that Garbutt should have a hand in the equalising goal which followed seventeen minutes later. After a quick run, he placed the ball with a square centre straight in front of goal, and after a quick scrimmage Holley pounced on the leather and beat Brownlie with a splendid fast drive.

And later in the same report:

After the interval this wing couple fell off somewhat; but Garbutt did excellently. He made many fine runs, but never selfishly stuck to the leather when it was his duty to part with it. His centres were well timed and skilfully executed, and if they could have been turned to account England would certainly not have been beaten.[9]

Beaten or not, as a patriotic Englishman, Garbutt cherished his medal and the memories that the day would provide him in his later life.

It was around this time that Garbutt met Dublin-born Anna Marie Stewart. An attractive woman of fair complexion, with deep, dark eyes, she was six years his junior. They quickly became inseparable, spending every possible moment together when Garbutt was not training or playing.

With consecutive top four finishes, Blackburn might have confidently expected to have kicked on and challenged for the Division One title. A twelfth place finish was foreseen by no one and was obviously a massive disappointment to everyone connected with the club. Rover's away form was largely to blame; they saved their solitary away win until the season's final game. Garbutt was virtually an ever-present in the side up until the 6-2 home win against Bury on 21 January 1911 in which he made his twenty-second and final appearance of the season. In its match report on the Monday after the game, *Athletic News* reported on Garbutt's injury:

> *Garbutt was prominent with some fast runs and some capital centres, and it was unfortunate when he had to leave the field , having strained a muscle of the groin.*[10]

Having tasted relative success, Blackburn's chairman, Lawrence Cotton, was greedy for more. Garbutt's injury had necessitated a replacement, so, after overcoming the competition of Newcastle United, John Simpson was signed from Falkirk for a then British record transfer fee of £1,800. Simpson's success in a Blackburn jersey would mean that Garbutt's star was on the wane. Like Garbutt, Simpson was an outside right and he was one of the best of his day. Born in Manchester on Christmas Day 1886 to Scottish parents, John (Jock) Simpson moved to Scotland as a young boy. His good form with Blackburn earned him an England debut against Ireland in February 1911, and he went on to make eight international appearances.

Garbutt played no further part in Blackburn's 1910–11 campaign and his situation did not improve by the start of the next season. This was to be a monumental season for Blackburn and Garbutt in different ways. Blackburn would win the First Division title for the first time and Garbutt would find himself plying his trade in another country and in a different capacity. The game against Notts County on 16 September 1911 was to be Garbutt's first of the season and the last of his career. Ironically, he was replacing the injured Simpson who, 'for the first time since he donned the Rovers jersey, had to stand down through injury, and thus Garbutt returned to his old place.'[11]

That Garbutt's career came to an end at the age of twenty-nine should perhaps not come as a complete surprise. He had suffered regular injuries throughout his playing days and obviously had no access to the physiotherapy and surgery that modern players receive.

Equally, being a player who posed a threat to the opposition, Garbutt was always liable to receive particular 'attention'.

As the sports historian Pierre Lanfranchi has written:

He was playing in an exposed position and was often fouled by strong full-backs who did not care how they stopped opposing wingers.[12]

While professional football offered a career path with obvious financial rewards to young men from working-class backgrounds, it 'could also be cruel to those … who suffered injury in what was, by late twentieth century standards, a primitive medical culture.'[13] It seems that when the injury occurred, Blackburn club officials were not fully aware of the severity, for in the following week, the local press reported:

W. Garbutt, who severely strained his muscles on Saturday, is progressing favourably, but it is not expected that he will able to turn out again for five or six weeks. The popular winger does not enjoy the best of luck.

Time would show this to be a hopelessly optimistic diagnosis. Despite the best available treatment and a number of attempts at a comeback, Garbutt was finally forced to accept the inevitable. His career as a top-flight footballer was over. He was never to pull on Blackburn's famous blue and white jersey in a competitive match again.

To add to William's concerns, Anna announced she was pregnant. Although overjoyed at the news, there can be no doubt that Garbutt would have endured sleepless nights worrying how he was going to provide for a wife and child. Being a professional footballer gave him a status he enjoyed, and wage he would find difficult to match outside of the game.

The English professional game was littered with ex-players forced out prematurely through injury. Looking for employment as a coach in the English game was not a viable option either. The role was not seen as particularly important, perhaps something to be carried out on a part-time basis along with secretarial duties.[14]

Despite the misgivings about his own career, Garbutt was an honourable man and asked Anna to marry him. She accepted his proposal and the two were married at Manchester Register Office on 29 November 1911, Anna giving her address as the Brunswick Hotel in Manchester's Piccadilly. William became a father when Anna gave birth to their son, Stuart Paul Garbutt, in Fylde on 15 April 1912. Just one month later Garbutt would accept the offer to become coach of Genoa. Later on 26 August 1912 *Athletic News* reported somewhat dismissively that five players had departed Blackburn Rovers at season's end, including 'Garbutt, who has gone coaching at Genoa'.

Chapter 2
The Move to Genova

Genoa Cricket & Athletic Club was founded on 7 September 1893 at a meeting attended by the British diplomat Sir Charles Alfred Payton and sundry other notables. At this stage Italians were not invited to become members. The first 'playing field' was granted to the side by two Scotsmen, Messrs Wilson and McLaren, who owned a factory in the Sampierdarena district of the city. Initially the club played cricket rather than football and would challenge the crews of the various ships that docked in the port of Genova.

All was to change in 1896 however when Dr James Richardson Spensley disembarked in Genova to take up the post of doctor to the crews of British ships in the Italian port. Thanks to his influence, football joined cricket on the list of pastimes and a year later Italians were finally admitted as members. Spensley fulfilled a number of roles, from goalkeeper of questionable ability, to director and referee.

Dubious ability or not, Spensley has six Italian championships with Genoa to his name. The first, more of a tournament than a championship, saw Genoa compete with three other teams, FC Torinese, Ginnastica di Torino and Internazionale di Torino, with Genoa triumphing over Internazionale di Torino 2-1 in the final. That first Genoa team deserves mention; Spensley, Leaver, Bocciardo, Dapples, Bertollo, Le Pelley, Ghiglione, Pasteur II, Ghigliotti, De Galleani and Baird. Already Italian footballers were beginning to make inroads into the bastion of Englishness that was Genoa Cricket and Football Club.

From 1898 to 1904 Genoa dominated the Italian championship, only Milan denying them a clean sweep with their victory in 1901. An indication, if any were needed, of the English influence over the infant Italian football, can be found in the fact that the word 'cricket' can be found in the title of nine out of the first ten champions (Genoa Cricket & Football Club winning six titles and Milan Cricket & Football Club winning on three occasions).[15]

After 1904 however, Genoa CFC went into a downward spiral and Pro Vercelli, a team fielding exclusively Italian players, began to dominate the championship, winning the title five times between 1908 and the 1912–13 season.

Aside from the general malaise at the Genoa club, two major factors made it imperative for their directors to seek an improvement on the pitch. The first was the construction of the impressive Marassi Stadium (opened on 14 July 1910 by an ambitious Genoa board), which was able to accommodate twenty-five thousand supporters. It was essential the side be successful if the Marassi was to be anywhere near full. Secondly, there was the fact that Genoa's local rivals, Andrea Doria, had finished two points above them in the 1910–11 season.

Genoa well and truly signalled their ambitions by appointing William Garbutt. What is less certain is how they spotted him for the post in the first place. One version has it that while living in England Vittorio Pozzo, (who would go on to become the manager of the victorious Italian national sides in the 1934 and 1938 World Cups and the 1936 Olympic football tournament in Berlin) saw Garbutt playing for Blackburn and recommended him to the Genovese as coach.

Writing in Italy's famous football weekly *Il Calcio Illustrato*, Pozzo reminisced on how he, while studying in England as a young man, would travel by train to the cities of the midlands and the north to watch a Saturday afternoon game of football. One of these excursions took him to Blackburn where he had taken in a match between Blackburn Rovers and Manchester United. Pozzo recounts how, with the first half coming to a close, Garbutt gathered the ball near to the touchline. Approaching his full-back, the tricky winger pushed the ball to the right of his opponent and made a movement to go on his opposite side. In an instant, Garbutt had fallen to the floor. Pozzo reports that, despite bravely attempting to return to the field, 'his career as a footballer was finished.'

As attractive as Pozzo's recollections might be, they cannot be accurate. The official registrations of Blackburn Rovers for the 1911–12 season, the originals of which are kept in the National Football Museum in Preston, show that Garbutt's one and only game for Rovers that season was against Notts County a fortnight before the Rovers–United tie witnessed by Pozzo. The sports journalist and author Brian Glanville somewhat embellishes the story further:

> One day, when Manchester United played Blackburn, the fair-haired, clever Blackburn outside-right was badly injured right in front of where Pozzo was standing. That player was Garbutt.
> Years later when Pozzo's Torino team was playing Genoa, Pozzo heard an English voice talking. He looked round – and there was Garbutt! Pozzo told him that he had seen him play his very last game: Garbutt was astounded.[16]

More likely is the version that sees Garbutt recommended to Genoa by the brother of Irishman Thomas Coggins, who ran Genoa's youth side. Either way, Garbutt was offered and accepted the post with little hesitation. While some have suggested that money was the main reason for Garbutt moving to Italy (Lanfranchi) there is no doubt that, throughout his career, Garbutt was something of a risk taker and adventurer. He managed the Genoa side that toured South America in 1923, and even after tasting success with Genoa, AS Roma and and Napoli in Italy, he plunged himself enthusiastically into another adventure by moving to Spain to manage Athletic Bilbao.

Contrast this with the view expressed by Cox, Russell and Vamplew in their *Encyclopedia of British Football*:

British footballers have not been good travellers. As well as the cultural and linguistic barriers to foreign settlement, few players have been inclined to leave the largest, most prestigious (and) best quality leagues in the world. Those Britons who have played abroad have tended to stay only for short spells and have generally been unable to integrate into the host culture.[17]

Garbutt's attitude towards the new experience on offer also contrasts sharply with that of the Football Association whose insularity and perceived superiority were to lead them to decline the world governing body's invitation to enter the 1930, 1934 and 1938 World Cup tournaments.

All this is not to suggest that money was unimportant to Garbutt, however. The facts stared him square in the face. He was, in his own terms, 'crocked', would never play professional football again and had a wife and young son to support. Professional football management was unheard of in England. Genoa seemed the perfect solution for all concerned.

It is important not to underestimate the step Garbutt was about to take. The world was a much bigger place in the early twentieth century and footballers and football managers were not the well-travelled men they became. The only way a young man of Garbutt's background would have normally had the opportunity to travel beyond the borders of his own country would have been by donning the King's uniform.

Garbutt was leaving Britain only weeks after the shocking news of the sinking of RMS *Titanic* in the north Atlantic. The nation he was leaving behind was going through something of a social upheaval. Respectable society was outraged at the window smashing antics of Emmeline Pankhurst and her suffragette followers, Herbert Asquith's Liberals had just introduced the Third Home Rule Bill in relation to Ireland and a six-week national strike observed by more than a million miners had recently ended. Compared with Garbutt's new home, however, Britain was a model of calm and stability.

In September of 1911, Italy had invaded Libya. Though this was a popular move among many sections of the Italian population[18] the aftermath of the war would lead to deep divisions within society. When the benefits of war failed to materialise and public unrest began to grow, the socialist movement was well positioned to take full advantage. The socialist newspaper *Avanti!* (edited by a certain Benito Mussolini) called openly for revolution.

For their part, the Italian right expressed dismay at the perceived weakness of Prime Minister Giolitti's Liberals in the face of the socialists and began to clamour for an authoritarian regime to right Italy's wrongs. The nation was polarising. The twenty-nine-year-old William Garbutt entered this maelstrom, stepping into the bright Genovese sunshine. Little could he or anyone else have imagined at this stage that his association with Italian football would end up being so long and distinguished.

This first sighting of Genova, with her busy port framed by the dramatic Ligurian Apennine mountain ranges, must have provided a stark contrast to Garbutt's Lancashire. A new language, a new culture, new colleagues, same game.

Initially, it was necessary for officials from Genoa to find a way to overcome Italian football's prohibition of professionalism within the sport. It was left to George Davidson, a club director, to explore ways in which Garbutt could receive his manager's salary without contravening the league's rules. In a country such as Italy, where rules and regulations such as these are viewed as a contest with the authorities, Davidson arranged for Garbutt to be paid via his business in a wide variety of creative ways, whether as a consultant, or by exaggerating and inflating receipts, expenses and the like. When Garbutt finally got to meet his players, there was an instant rapport.

The language barrier was not as difficult to over-come as the new coach may have been fearing. There was a sizeable contingent of British players and the Swiss could translate for the Italians. It was the common language of football that bound the squad to-gether, however, and all the Genoa players would have been more than aware of Garbutt's accomplish-ments in the English professional game. They looked up to him, eager to learn from someone who had competed successfully among the game's elite for a number of seasons. Garbutt had listened well as a player, observing the training regimes and tactics employed by the various trainers he had played under. He looked to build and improve upon these and to pass them on to his new charges.

There was no area of the Genoa club's approach and preparation that Garbutt could not improve. He duly set about the task ahead of him with energy and enthusiasm. From the very outset, Garbutt's task would have been to improve the morale of a side that had performed poorly the season prior to his appointment. Remember that this campaign had seen Genoa fall behind their rivals Andrea Doria for the very first time.

Even in the early days of Italian football, local rivalry was fierce and every member of the Genoa squad would have been keen to ensure that this was not repeated. Prior to Garbutt's arrival, training sessions would have been fairly haphazard, largely unstructured and without aim. All this was to change. The physical fitness of the players was now paramount and Garbutt placed great emphasis upon this.

The players may have been bemused upon seeing cones strategically placed around the training ground with the expectation that they would dribble the ball in and out of them, left foot then right, improving their ball control with every session. Every aspect of the game, from tackling to heading, things that came as second nature to an English professional but needed to be taught to these willing scholars, received attention.

Garbutt's players, despite the strenuous physical demands that were being placed on them, often for the first time, looked to him with the utmost affection and respect. He was not a manager who felt the need to raise his voice to his players. He recognised this as self-defeating and enjoyed a good relationship with his players without ever losing his authority. Again drawing upon his experience of the English game, Garbutt took complete control of team affairs. Prior to his appointment, team selection would have emerged as a decision made by a committee, consisting probably of the team captain and various directors. Garbutt point blank refused to acquiesce to such a process. On the field matters were his domain and his alone.

Before long, Garbutt came to be known to his players by the English term 'Mister' a label that is used by players of Italian football clubs to this day when discussing their manager. This is no mean achievement. Italian football has always been keen to exert its independence from its (albeit contested) English traditions, a trend which has even found its way into the terminology of the game. Hence, corner becomes 'calcio di angolo,' free kick 'calcio di punizione', offside 'fuori gioco' and penalty 'calcio di rigore'. From Garbutt's day to this, however, the manager remains the 'Mister'.

Garbutt arranged a number of 'friendly' games in September and October to give him an opportunity to see his charges in action. The season, and Garbutt's career as a football manager, began in earnest, however, on 3 November 1912 at the Arena Civica in Milan with Internazionale as the opposition. Like many ex-players who go on to manage, Garbutt was not comfortable in watching from the sidelines, at least in the early days. One can imagine him kicking every ball, challenging for every header as he had been doing competitively only months earlier. The new coach found it strange walking among his players in the dressing room before the game, joining in their chatter designed to disguise pre-match nerves, and not taking part in the ritual of donning his playing kit. He glanced absent-mindedly at his watch countless times awaiting the kick-off. On this particular occasion, he was able to walk up to the touchline but no further and led his team to a sweet 3-2 victory.

He had good reason at the final whistle to give a special pat on the back to his compatriot and centre forward, John Wylie Grant, whose hat-trick ensured the win. The first home game for Garbutt was played a week later at the Marassi stadium and resulted in an emphatic 6-0 drubbing of local rivals Andrea Doria. Despite the easy win, Garbutt must have admired two of the Andrea Doria players, Enrico Sardi and Aristodemo Santamaria, as they were to join Genoa some time later (thereby triggering one of the many crises to affect the Italian game down the years).

Four straight victories were followed by the first defeat, away to Milan on 19 January 1913. The Milan line-up that day included one Renzo De Vecchi, who would go on to become known as 'il figlio di Dio' (the son of God) by an adoring Italian public.

Garbutt instantly recognised talent and ability and in his first handful of games as manager he had already identified Sardi, Santamaria and De Vecchi as players he wanted in his Genoa team.

Genoa's seven victories from ten games saw them qualify for the *Girone Finale*, a regional play-off to determine who would play in the final. Two defeats to Pro Vercelli, the eventual champions, proved costly to Genoa, however, and they were duly knocked out.

This first season in charge would probably have been something of a disappointment to Garbutt. He had high expectations of himself and his players and was certainly looking to make more of an impact upon the Italian game. The 1912–13 season did represent an improvement on the previous campaign, however, and would have given him a good indication of those positions that he would need to strengthen if his side was to be truly competitive and the subsequent signing of De Vecchi from Milan can surely be seen as laying the foundations for Genoa's success (three championships) over the next twelve years or so. De Vecchi made his debut for Italy at the tender age of sixteen years, three months and twenty-three days old. He was small (163cms) for a footballer, yet can be considered as a 'modern' defender, in that he was tough, fast and possessed great tactical awareness.

Little wonder then that Garbutt had little trouble persuading Genoa's president George Davidson to pay Milan twenty-four thousand lire (around £24,000) to part with the nineteen-year-old. Once again, Genoa needed to find a means by which to circumvent the rules prohibiting professionalism. In De Vecchi's case, they would achieve this by making him Italy's most highly paid footballing bank clerk. Considered by many as a true gentleman of the game, De Vecchi was sent off only once in seventeen seasons playing for Genoa and that in a game against Juventus when the referee Signor Varisco found dubious cause to send off two other Genoa players as well.

Chapter 3
From Football to Fighting

Garbutt decided to make good use of the contacts he had made during his career in the English game by inviting his first professional club, Reading FC, to tour northern Italy at the end of the 1912–13 season. At this stage, Reading were in the first division of the Southern League. Reading took up the offer and fourteen players and four club officials began an exhausting schedule of five games in only nine days. They played not only the top club sides of the day but also the Italian national side.

After a day of travelling by train and ferry, the Reading team arrived in Genova and played the first game of their tour a day later, on 11 May 1913, Garbutt's Genoa providing the opposition. History shows that the English side won this game 4-2. Both Genoa's goals that day were scored by their Italian international forward Attilio Fresia. He must have impressed the watching Reading officials for he was signed by the Berkshire club and went on to become the first Italian to play professional football in England.

Even though Garbutt's career had not long ended,

it appears that he avoided the temptation to play against his former team and settled for refereeing the game. Reading followed up the victory over Genoa with further wins against Milan (5-0), Pro Vercelli (6-0) and a win against an Italian 'Select XI' (2-0). They suffered one defeat on the tour, against Casale (2-1) in their third game of five. The reverse has been blamed (perhaps a little unsportingly) on the fact that Casale's pitch was so small.

The fact that the cream of Italian club sides and the Italian national team had been brushed aside by Reading, an English Southern league side, provides a telling insight into the gulf that existed in footballing terms between the two nations in 1913. All the more amazing then that in the space of only a quarter of a century, Italy would go on to win the World Cup twice (in 1934 and 1938) and be crowned as Olympic champions in 1936. The foundations that Garbutt was laying with Genoa at this time would play no small part in their success.

Genoa, with Renzo De Vecchi making his first competitive appearance for the team, opened the 1913–14 season with a 3-3 home draw against Torino. Once again, Genoa's fourteen victories from eighteen games would see them qualify for the *Girone Finale*. This season, however, Casale would prove to be Garbutt's nemesis. Three defeats in four tussles against them would prove to be Genoa's undoing and Casale went on to win the championship against Lazio.

Garbutt could have been forgiven for having only one eye on his job at this time. Competing with football as the main topic of conversation was the worsening relationships between the main powers of Europe. Each letter that arrived from relatives and friends back in England gave him the latest news, each daily newspaper detailing how the intricate pattern of alliances between the nations would lead them to topple, domino-like, into global conflict.

Even so, Garbutt was numbed to learn that Great Britain, in line with its treaty with Belgium, had declared war on Germany on 4 August 1914. Just as his work with Genoa appeared to be bringing positive results it seemed as if the whole edifice was about to come crashing down around them all.

Garbutt was faced with a dilemma. Should he return home to serve his country or remain in Genova and continue his work in football? (Conscription was not introduced in Britain until January 1916 and even then for single men only.) The fact that Italy did not enter the war in 1914 may have helped to sway Garbutt's decision. As a member of the Triple Alliance with Austria and Hungary, Italy might well have been expected to have entered the war alongside her alliance partners. However, some intricate political manoeuvring by Prime Minister Giolitti ensured that Italian neutrality was assured for the time being at least.

The Italians were busy negotiating with Great Britain, France and Russia and the Alliance to ensure the best possible 'deal' for the country when the war ended. So far as football was concerned the jigsaw was slowly but surely coming together to Garbutt's satisfaction. Even the loss of John Wylie Grant, the prolific goal scorer who had given Garbutt and

Genoa such sterling service in his two seasons, was not as damaging as it might have been, as it merely provided the coach with an opportunity to strengthen his team. Sardi and Santamaria were duly poached from neighbours Andrea Doria, tempted no doubt by the handsome one thousand lire signing on-fee dangled before each of them (this at a time when the average daily wage for a working male in the north of Italy would have been two or three lire per day).[19]

The story goes that Sardi and Santamaria had the misfortune (or naivety) to present their signing-on cheques to a bank teller who was an avid fan of Andrea Doria. He, miffed at witnessing his side's two best players depositing their thirty pieces of silver, promptly reported the suspect transaction to the relevant authorities. In the ensuing legal case, the hawks of the Italian football federation called for Genoa Cricket & Football Club to be wound up and for Sardi and Santamaria to receive life bans. This was later reduced to a two-year ban. Only the expert and timely intervention of Edoardo Pasteur (associated with the club from its earliest days, he won six championships and later became the club's president) saw Genoa rescued from this potential catastrophe and the ban was lifted on both club and players. Nevertheless, the whole episode was the cause of a great deal of anxiety for Garbutt. Here he was, having uprooted his family and living far from home, trying to forge a career in a new environment, and faced with having it all taken away from him. The 'creative' manner in which De Vecchi, Sardi and

Santamaria were all signed for Genoa proves that neither the club nor Garbutt were afraid to bend the existing rules in order to strengthen the team. Pity Andrea Doria. They were to get an early opportunity to regret Sardi and Santamaria's departure when Genoa beat them in a pre-season *Coppa Lombardia* match. Just to rub salt into their wounds, two goals from Sardi plus further strikes from Santamaria, Wallsingham and Leale gave Genoa an easy 5-0 win.

Evidence, if any were needed, that Garbutt was highly respected within the game, came when Vittorio Pozzo, the coach of the Italian national side, invited him to travel with the squad to Switzerland and assist him in the preparation of the team for a friendly international. Two Genoa players were in the team, the impeccable De Vecchi and Casanova, who was tragically killed in the forthcoming global conflict. The game, played on the 17 May, 1914, was won by the Italians with a solitary goal from Casale player Barbesino.

With the attacking prowess Garbutt now had at his disposal, Genoa found goals easy to come by. The first game of the 1914–15 season saw them thrash hapless Acqui 16-0! Garbutt's side were well and truly beginning to gel. Andrea Doria were beaten both home and away, 3-0 and 8-0 respectively. In this latter game played on 22 November 1914, Andrea Doria tempers flared as they were put to the sword. One can only imagine the humiliation felt by the players. Defeated heavily, not only by fierce rivals, the wounds were inflicted by former team-mates, with Santamaria helping himself to two goals and Sardi one. Reports suggest that the game was abandoned after eighty minutes when the referee, Signor Gregori, ordered three Doria players to leave the field of play. Once again Genoa qualified easily for the *Girone Finale*. On 18 April 1915 they drew 1-1 away to Milan.

This was followed up a week later with a resounding 5-3 triumph at home to Internazionale. As the club prepared for its away game against Vittorio Pozzo's Torino at Campo Stupinigi on 2 May 1915, nobody could have foreseen that the result would rock the club to its very core and test Garbutt's self-confidence to its very limit. By half-time, Genoa were already 3-0 down. At the end of the game, they had lost 6-1, a meaningless consolation goal scored by Santamaria.

The eleven Genoa men trudged disconsolately from the pitch, their heads bowed. Garbutt was shell-shocked, and questioned his team selection, his tactics, his preparation. This was the biggest reverse to date in his short managerial career. Once over the initial shock, Garbutt's professional instinct took over and he began contemplating and preparing for the all-important tussle in the home tie against Milan the following week.

Garbutt made two changes to the line-up. Barabino, a defender, and Benvenuto were dropped and replaced by Leale and Wallsingham. Garbutt's amendments were to prove justified and his team beat Milan 3-0 with goals from Wallsingham, Berardo and, from the penalty spot, De Vecchi. Faith, in his own ability and that of the players, was restored. Two *Girone Finale* games remained for Genoa; away to Internazionale and a home tie against Torino. Garbutt looked forward keenly to this final game as an opportunity to erase the bad memories of the earlier encounter. On the 16 May 1915, Garbutt's Genoa took to Internazionale's Campo via Galdoni pitch and duly won 3-1 with goals from Santamaria, Wallsingham and Berardo.

Although unaware at the time, this would prove to be the last time that Garbutt would manage his men until after the Great War. Some of the players he was destined never to see again. Although Austria–Hungary had made some concessions to Italian territorial demands, these did not include the Italian-speaking Trentino or the city of Trieste. The Entente promised not only Trentino and Trieste but other Austrian territory. The die was cast and in April 1915, the Italian Foreign Minister, Sonnino, without the knowledge of the Italian Parliament, signed the Treaty of London. One month later, on 24 May 1915, Italy declared war on Austria.

The Italian Football Federation made the momentous decision to cancel the remaining fixtures when notified of Italy's entry into the conflict. Torino and Internazionale, both on five points, could mathematically have equalled Genoa's points tally, and yet, amid great controversy, the 1914–15 championship was awarded 'posthumously' to Genoa Cricket & Football Club, their seventh Italian league title and William Garbutt's first as a manager.

It was certainly not the manner in which he would have liked his team to become champions, but more pressing concerns were paramount now. His work in Italy, for the time being at least, completed,

Garbutt bade a sorrowful farewell to all at Genoa and returned to England with Anna and Stuart. The future, not only for the Garbutts but also for Europe and the world was shrouded in uncertainty.

Garbutt helped Anna and Stuart down from the train as it pulled into Victoria Station. The sight that met them may well have been expected but it both astonished and impressed them nonetheless. The entire length of the platform was a carpet of khaki uniforms, with troops heading for the front bidding farewell to their loved ones. William and Anna both knew that they would be re-enacting this exact same scene in due course, where those leaving put on a show of joviality and those being left behind did their best to hide their obvious concerns. The trio made their way north to the familiar streets of Lancashire to stay with family. No sooner had they arrived than it seemed that William was striding determinedly up the steps of the town hall in Ashton under Lyne where, on 7 July 1915 he signed the oath to serve his country in what would become known as the Great War. Aged thirty-two years and six months, and giving his occupation as 'footballer', Garbutt signed the following allegiance:

I, William Garbutt, swear by Almighty God, that I will be faithful and bear true allegiance to His Majesty King George the Fifth, His Heirs and Successors, and that I will, as in duty bound, honestly and faithfully defend His Majesty, His Heirs and Successors, in Person, Crown and dignity against all enemies and will observe and obey all orders of His Majesty, His Heirs and Successors, and of the Generals and Officers set over me. So help me God.

As with literally hundreds of thousands of fellow Britons, Garbutt had answered Lord Kitchener's call to enlist and in so doing had become a soldier in 'A' Battery, 181st Brigade (Ashton under Lyne Regiment) of the Royal Field Artillery. In time, this brigade would become part of the 40th Division that was formed between September and December 1915. The 40th would be made up of 'bantam' and other units, consideration being given to men who failed to meet the regulation height of five feet three inches. Many of those who came forward were considered unfit for active service. The necessary weeding-out process held up the training programme; in turn the division was not considered ready to make its way to the front until late spring 1916 at the very earliest. Just how necessary and drastic this weeding out became is evidenced by the fact that one battalion joining the division at Aldershot with more than a thousand men, had been decimated after medical rejections to not much more than two hundred accepted for active service.[20]

After accepting the 'King's shilling' Garbutt made the journey home to Anna and Stuart. Within a couple of days he had received his joining instructions and travel warrant. Garbutt had previous military experience (with the 99th Battery of the Royal Field Artillery) and of leading and motivating men. Unlike many of the poor physical specimens that had signed up to serve, he was fit from his coaching work with Genoa and enjoyed a diet that the average working-class Briton could only have dreamt of. Little surprise then that he rose rapidly through the ranks, gaining promotion to corporal only three weeks after joining up. Just two months after signing up, Garbutt had been promoted to acting sergeant.

Compared with their German foe and French Allies, the British Army had been hopelessly ill prepared for the battles ahead. Within a week of the declaration of war, Germany had 3.8 million well-trained men in uniform. By August 1914, the British force stood at a little over 247,000. France could call upon 823,000 regular soldiers from the outset, a figure which was bolstered by almost three million reservists by the end of August 1914. Britain's six infantry divisions paled into insignificance when compared with Germany's eighty-seven. Though conscription was politically unpalatable to Asquith's Liberals, there could be no denying the need for a massive expansion in numbers of men in uniform if they were to successfully overcome the ruthlessly efficient machine that was the German army.

In response, Kitchener began his campaign to recruit men to his 'New Army', his pointing finger and staring eyes peering down from thousands of posters. Army recruitment offices were inundated by men willing to serve. 'Pals' battalions were formed as the authorities recognised that men would be more likely to sign up and fight alongside men from their own community or trade.

The government established additional offices for men to sign; in police stations, factories and the like. Recruitment stations were set up in village halls in rural areas to enable men to join with the minimum of delay.

The massive surge in the numbers joining up led to other problems. There was a drastic shortage of uniforms to go around, 'the majority of men joining the New Army remained in their own clothing for many weeks'.[21]

The shortages extended to basic equipment such as guns and ammunition:

> ... *the artillery in particular suffered greatly in its training programme: with every available gun being sent to France, there was simply nothing left for the New Army gunners to learn their trade.*[22]

For almost a year Garbutt and thousands of his comrades were either spared or denied, depending upon your point of view, the journey across the English Channel to the Western Front. Military service for them would consist of nothing more exciting than endless rounds of 'square bashing' or other exercises designed to prepare them for the battles to come.

In late May 1916, however, William received the news that he knew must come sooner or later; he would leave for France on 1 June. The remaining days passed in a whirl before Anna accompanied William to Southampton docks. One can only imagine the scene, acted out by thousands upon thousands, day after day; mothers, fathers, sisters, brothers, wives and children, all bidding a tearful farewell to their loved ones. Garbutt waved goodbye to his family from the deck of the cross-channel steamer, *La France*.

A good many of those troops who set sail for France must have been embarking on their first ever sea voyage if Whitton's account of the history of the 40th Division is anything to go by. He accorded a great deal of sympathy to the crew of the steamer for the large quantity of vomit that they needed to clean off the deck.

At three in the morning on 2 June, William and his fellow troops reached Le Havre and anxiously awaited the order to disembark. This arrived some four hours later and the men began the first of many marches on foreign soil, inland towards a holding station near to Béthune. If the gravity of the situation had yet to dawn on William and his brothers-in-arms, surely it did when they were instructed to complete their last will and testament. Garbutt's is dated 27 June 1916 and reads thus:

> *In the event of my*
> *death I give the whole*
> *of my property & effects*
> *to my wife Anna Garbutt*
> *Duke of Wellington*
> *William St. Woolwich.*
> *Sergt. W. Garbutt*
> *27.6.16*
> *Noeux-les-Mines*

At that time Noeux-les-Mines was one of many towns in the Pas de Calais region given over to mining and as such could never be described as picturesque. Whitton summed it up thus:

> *Noeux-les-Mines was a dreary-looking town with wide footways at either side of the main road, the latter being pavé of the usual vileness and the former simply beaten-down mud and coal dust kept in place by a narrow whitewashed stone kerb.*[23]

The howitzer brigade that Garbutt was a part of was situated in the village of Bully Grenay, 'one of the most extraordinary villages to be found on the whole front'.[24]

Bully Grenay was remarkable for the simple fact that it was situated within the battle zone. Indeed, in spite of having British Army howitzers camped within their back gardens, most inhabitants had stayed in their homes, for the time being at least. Despite being only three thousand yards from the front line, most windows were still intact.

The months of July and August passed by largely without incident for Garbutt and his comrades; the most noteworthy moment for him came when he was officially confirmed in the rank of sergeant on 19 August 1916.

Weeks and month passed and as the conflict approached Christmas 1916 the 40th Division made its way by road and rail towards the front line between Bouchavesnes and Rancourt in the Somme.

Considering that Garbutt had joined up in July 1915, one might be tempted to conclude that he and his fellow troops had enjoyed an easy passage from that date to this. All was about to change however, and it is worth quoting Whitton at length to paint a picture of the hellish conditions that the 40th Division were confronted with during this passage of the war.

Now began three months in the most God-forsaken and miserable area in France, bar, possibly, the salient of Ypres.

The whole countryside was a churned-up yeasty mass of mud, as a result of the vile weather and of the battle which even yet had not petered out. The weather was awful. Constant rain was varied by spells of intensely cold weather and some very heavy snowfalls. Mud and dirt were everywhere. The French had been in occupation of the line, and, however gallant our allies may have been, their notions on sanitation were mediaeval.

Billets in the back area were camps of dirty, wet and decrepit huts. Seen at that period of the year the countryside was bleak, mournful, uninviting and miserable: roads cut up; villages badly knocked about, and everywhere 'signs of the advance of large bodies of troops' and French troops at that. So much for the back area, Bray to Corlu. But no pen can do justice to the front region – it could not be called a 'line'.

It just beggars description, consisting of a mess of shell holes; a general sea of mud; lesser lakes and lagoons of icy water. Trenches did not exist, except for short lengths on higher ground; of communication trenches there were none; men had to do the best they could to improve such shell holes 'as were least full of water and other more unpleasant relics of the battle.' Villages there were in profusion, on the map; but in reality they were but flattened brickwork. Looking back on those days it is hard to realise how human beings could have existed in such conditions. The only cheering thought was that the enemy might be as badly off as, or even worse off than, the 40th Division, for the ground sloped badly for them; they, however, were on ground that had not been fought over, so that, save for the disadvantages of the lie of the ground, they were in comparative comfort.[25]

Not only had the men suffered. Exhausted, pack-laden horses often became stuck in the quagmire and had to be shot if they suffered a broken leg or some similar mishap. Sentimentality towards the animals reduced in direct relation to the men's own misery, however. Not even Christmas Day 1916 brought respite for the men as they were subjected to a three-hour artillery barrage by the German army.

And in these conditions of strafe, mud, wet, dirt, discomfort, cold and trench feet the 40th Division completed its first six months in France.[26]

Being a professional soldier, William's immediate concern would have been to ensure his own safety, then that of his fellow soldiers. Every soldier in the trenches was aware of the danger of sniper fire and of the need to keep their heads beneath the parapet.

In quieter moments his thoughts would have returned to his wife and child, and like every man on both sides of the conflict, he yearned to return to the arms and embraces of his loved ones. Little did Garbutt know at this stage, but his return to England was not too far away. There was still a good deal of discomfort ahead of him, however, related once more to the prevailing weather conditions rather than to those created by battle.

The conditions on the Somme described by Whitton inclined against any serious military operations during this period but another enemy, the cold, continued to pose a real threat. From around 12 February, a cold spell set in, which lasted for about a week, 'the temperature at times falling to nearly zero Fahrenheit'[27] (almost -18°C).

For some time, Garbutt's superiors had taken note of his ability to lead men and decided to recommend him for an appointment as a Temporary Officer. This entailed him returning home for officer training at one of the cadet training schools which had been especially set up for the purpose. The British army's officer class had already been small when compared with those of the French and German armies. Its numbers had been decimated by various battles and had to be replenished somehow. For the first time there was a real opportunity for men of working-class backgrounds to attain officer rank and Garbutt fitted the bill perfectly.

And so, no doubt elated to be returning home, but with an air of sadness at leaving behind the friendships forged during training and in the heat of battle over the previous nineteen months, William Garbutt bade farewell to his comrades and set sail for England on 15 February 1917. Shortly after arriving home, Garbutt lodged his official application for a temporary commission within the British army.

His application provided the three referees requested; in Garbutt's case these were Lawrence Cotton, mill owner and chairman of Blackburn Rovers Football Club (who became Mayor of Blackburn in this year), Captain Colin West, Garbutt's superior from his days in the 181st Brigade, and the headmaster from his days as a pupil at Norbury School. The application stressed that it would not be possible to guarantee a posting to any particular regiment but did offer applicants the opportunity to indicate a preference. Garbutt requested only that he be allowed to continue to serve in the Royal Field Artillery.

His application duly accepted, Garbutt undertook his officer training at the No. 1 Officer Cadet School based in St. John's Wood, London, one of many such centres up and down the country . His training began on 30 March 1917 and some four months later, on 11 August, Garbutt received his commission at a ceremony attended by a proud Anna. He was a natural officer. He had been leading men since taking up the post of coach at Genoa in 1912. He cajoled, nursed and bullied men into battle every week and all his players gave their utmost for him. In addition, he simply looked the part of a British army officer.

Photographs of him in Genova show a man always well turned out in expensive tailored suits, polished shoes and a bowler hat. Equally impressive in his military uniform, he looked every inch the perfect English officer with his hair parted down the centre and sporting a clipped moustache. He was distinctly debonair.

The war had the effect of accelerating social change in Britain. As well as officers no longer being drawn exclusively from a public school elite, women had begun to replace men working in factories, ensuring the supply of munitions to the front line. Criticism at home with regard to the prosecution of the war by army generals was fundamental in making Britain a less deferential society than it had hitherto been.

Furthermore, the price of the acquiescence of the trades unions had been the guarantee of a voice and greater influence for that movement in any post-war Britain. Approximately 73,000 men gained temporary commissions via the Officer Cadet Schools with an increasing number of them coming 'through the ranks' as the months passed.

Though the cadet school was based in St John's Wood, training often took place on the hallowed turf of the nearby Lord's Cricket Ground. Garbutt and his fellow officers-to-be could often be found carrying out their gun drills at one or other end of the pitch.

The men with whom Garbutt was sharing a dormitory came from a rich variety of backgrounds. There were those like himself, experienced troops who had been serving at the front and had been recommended by superiors for officer training, youngsters who had just reached the age of military service, and others still who had up to now been working in one of the civilian professions or occupations considered by the authorities as being indispensable to the war effort.

One wonders how many of the horrors of life in the trenches that Garbutt had already witnessed he shared with the naïve, impressionable young men he was living among. While on parade, William wore his regular uniform with the addition of a white band around the rim of his hat, which marked him out as future officer material.

As training progressed however, Garbutt and those others who were coming up to the mark were sent to a firm of military tailors in Bond Street to be measured up for their new uniforms. Garbutt anxiously awaited news of his posting. It arrived soon enough. He was ordered to return to France to serve as a Second Lieutenant in the 186th Brigade of the 39th Division. On 3 September 1917, he received news of his commission via the following correspondence, from the war office:

… appoint you to be an Officer in our Special Reserve of Officers from the twelfth day of August 1917. You are therefore carefully and diligently to discharge your duties as such in the rank of Second Lieutenant.

Having been at home for almost a year now, leaving his wife and family yet again was a wrench for William, but he had never been the type to shirk his duties to his country and would not do so now. And so, on 7 December 1917, he set sail once again for France to join his new brigade who were based near Passchendale. Though almost a year had passed since William had left his comrades in the 40th Division, the scenery had changed barely at all.

In his *Short History of the 39th Divisional Artillery 1915–1918*, Wiebkin writes:

> *The ground in the vicinity of the battery positions was simply one mass of shell craters filled with liquid mud, and it was practically impossible to move a single gun from its position.*[28]

The next few months passed by in a haze of attack and counter-attack, the allies and their enemies engaged in a stand-off, gaining and losing by turn barren, wasted land that could be measured in yards. In March 1918, Germany's General Ludendorff launched his spring offensive, designed to drive a wedge between the British and French forces near Amiens. Initial gains were so promising for the German forces that Kaiser Wilhelm II was moved to declare 24 March a national holiday.

A lack of military hardware meant that the Germans were unable to follow up the initial successes, however. A month later, Garbutt was busy with his usual tasks, inspecting his troops, doing his best to keep up the morale of men by now heartily tired of the war and desperate to return to their families and former lives.

Living under fire was an occupational hazard and men of all ranks were injured on a regular basis. The day Garbutt's name would be added to the long list of casualties was 9 April. On this occasion the drone of the artillery in the field sounded different, somehow closer and more threatening. A blinding flash was followed by the impact of the aftershock, mud and debris flying in all directions. Garbutt, lying face down in the trench, could hear little other than the muffled shouts and screams of the men around him, running around in an understandable panic. Garbutt felt the warm blood seeping under the trouser leg of his uniform and required medical attention for shrapnel wounds to his left leg.

Fortunately for him the wounds were not overly serious and after a short period of recuperation he was back in uniform. With the entry of the Americans into the conflict, the writing was very much on the wall for Germany. Within four weeks of the allied 'Hundred Days Offensive' beginning on 8 August 1918, over one hundred thousand Germans had been taken prisoner. One hundred and twenty thousand allied troops and 414 tanks advanced some seven miles into German-held territory in only a matter of hours. Morale in both the German army and among the public at home was at a low ebb. Ration cuts and the impending military defeat made mutiny all the more likely.

The Kaiser began to look for an honourable means to extricate the nation from the war and attempted to broker a peace deal but none was forthcoming. After finally accepting the inevitable, the Kaiser abdicated on 9 November 1918 with the Armistice being signed two days later. Almost two months later, on the very final day of 1918, William Garbutt was on his way back to England to resume whatever life on Civvy Street had to offer him.

In common with many of the returning 'Tommies', Garbutt mourned for those of his colleagues who would not return and railed against the futility of war. Yet he was proud of his medals, the British War Medal and the Victory Medal, the ribbon of which he was entitled to adorn with two silver oak leaves, as a result of being 'Mentioned in Despatches' in the *London Gazette* by Field Marshal Sir Douglas Haig for actions 'deserving of special attention'.[29]

He was equally proud of the certificate sent to him in Haig's name and signed by the then Secretary of State for War, Winston Churchill. Dated 16 March 1919, the certificate reads: 'For gallant and distinguished services in the field. I have it in command from the King to record His Majesty's high appreciation of the services rendered.'

And so, with the signing of the Treaty of Versailles, the greatest conflict the world had witnessed finally came to an end. The cost in every way imaginable, but especially in human terms, had been huge.

Great Britain and her Empire had contributed almost nine million men to the war effort. A little short of a million had been slaughtered; more than two million were wounded. More than one in three who had signed up to serve had ended up as a casualty, not including those who returned home with psychological problems. Garbutt's 'adopted' country of Italy had paid an immense price also. Five and a half million had been mobilised; 650,000 made the ultimate sacrifice.

On 23 September 1919, the footballing authorities awarded the title for the 1914–15 season to Genoa Cricket & Football Club. Tragically, it was a title that a number of the team would be unable to celebrate, having been killed in action. Luigi Ferraris, who had represented Genoa from 1909–1912, goalkeeper Adolfo Gnecco, Claudio Casanova, Carlo Marassi and forward Alberto Sussone all died. And Virgilio Fossati, captain of both Internazionale and the Italian national team, had perished.

Perhaps the man who was most closely associated with Genoa, Doctor James Richardson Spensley, had lost his life while bravely tending to an injured German soldier. It must have felt as if the war had torn the very heart out of Genoa CFC. For their part, the Genoa directors were keen to regain Garbutt's services as coach of the team and to return to the format they had enjoyed before the outbreak of the conflict.

Garbutt received a telegram from Genoa on 12 August 1919 enquiring as to his intentions with regard to a return. Negotiations continued for two weeks after which time Genoa accepted the terms and conditions Garbutt had laid down. Upon resumption of his duties as coach, he received a healthy pay rise to the then princely sum of eight thousand lire per annum (approximately £24,000 at the 1920 exchange rate). In all likelihood, Garbutt would have returned to the helm without this financial incentive. Throughout his career he was never particularly adept at negotiating the best financial deal for himself despite his undoubted professional successes.

He had little hesitation in returning to Italy. Despite the assurances of the politicians, post-war Britain was not a land fit for returning heroes let alone professional football coaches. The English game was no more likely to provide a living to an ex-player now that hostilities had ceased than it had been before the war.

Chapter 4
Welcomed back

The city of Genova and Genoa Football Club and its players, supporters and officials welcomed back Garbutt as they would one of their own. Crucially, Anna was also happy to return to Genova with her husband. She suffered badly from asthma and the air in Genova suited her far better than that to be found in either Lancashire or London. Prior to the war, the sociable Mrs Garbutt had made a wide circle of friends in the city, not only among the British expatriates but also with the native Italians.

The Italy the Garbutts returned to in 1919 was not at peace with itself, however. The territorial gains promised to Italy in return for her support during the war failed to materialise.

The economy was burdened with massive debts and spiralling inflation. Companies such as Pirelli and Fiat that were strategic to the Italian war effort and thus able to gorge themselves on the government's military expenditure (Fiat increasing its capital from seventeen million lire in 1914 to two hundred million in 1919)[30] would now see their profits slashed due to government spending cuts.

Industrial militancy increased due to the workers' anger at cuts in real wages.

Membership of socialist trade unions increased eight-fold during the period 1918–1920. Politics was rapidly polarising between socialists advocating a Bolshevik-style revolution and the Nationalists representing the interests of the middle classes, industrialists and landowners. When Britain and the United States of America went back on their word and refused to agree to Italy's territorial claims to Fiume, the Nationalists' cries of a 'mutilated victory' began to gain credence.

Those soldiers returning from the war to be met with unemployment questioned if their valour had been worth the effort. An opportunist journalist by the name of Mussolini noted with interest how Gabriele D'Annunzio, a nationalist intellectual and poet, had marched into Fiume with two thousand armed men and occupied it in defiance of the government. Decisive, direct action had achieved more than endless government negotiating and the deaths of more than half a million Italians.

Shortly after Garbutt had arrived back in Genova, Benito Mussolini called the inaugural meeting of the *Fasci di Combattimento* on 23 March 1919. Some fifty 'rag-bag of futurists, anarchists, communists, syndicalists, republicans, Catholics, nationalists and liberals of various kinds'[31] attended the meeting. Employers in the urban centres were becoming increasingly concerned with what they saw as the growing radicalism of their workforce and feared that a Russian-style revolution was imminent. Landowners in the countryside felt the same. Mussolini and his black-shirted followers offered them the protection they felt the Liberal Government did not and local fascist gangs were employed to burn down the offices of the socialists and beatings of trades unionists were commonplace. Dangerous times lay ahead.

The fact that Garbutt was now living overseas did not prevent him from keeping abreast of events in Britain, particularly with regard to football. He had copies of the northern sports weekly *Athletic News* mailed to Genova and corresponded with that publication when his interest was grabbed by an article on the role of the coach in football. The article, headlined 'Garbutt on necessity of Coaches' reads as follows:

Readers will remember William Garbutt the plucky and skilfull outside right of Blackburn Rovers; the forward who, with such good grace, gave way to John Simpson, when he joined the Ewood Park eleven. Garbutt has been reading the articles of 'Tityrus' on the necessity of coaching even the best of teams and he writes us from Genoa the following letter:

Dear Tityrus, I do not think there are many young league players, or old ones for that matter, who would not welcome a coach instead of a trainer. The popular opinion was, and is, I believe, with trainers that their work consisted of keeping a player fit. I myself was under Paley, Dunmore and Bob Holmes, and never received any tips on how to play from any of them. Surely Bob Holmes, with his experience, might have thought it advisable to impart a little of his knowledge to young players – and the Rovers had a good few at that time. Anyhow, on getting 'crocked' the doctor told me I should not be fit to play first class football again. So I immediately took a position offered as coach to the Genoa Club here. That was in 1912. I remained with them until April 1915. Then I left to join the Service. After three years in France, I am back again feeling very fit and strip four or five times weekly, teaching the local men how the game should be played.

After reading your articles on the subject I also wondered why one has to come abroad to teach football, when there are none, or very few, coaches employed in England – the home of football. Football in Italy is going great guns. Clubs are springing up like mushrooms all over the place. The best clubs are about of the Lancashire Combination class, and visiting teams from home, including Reading, all suffered defeat here. I should like to see a First Division club out here this summer, a team who would play serious football and teach the Italians something. I have been asked by my club to make some enquiries; so perhaps we may be lucky, and to get a good side out.[32]

Once back in Genova with his family, Garbutt met with the Genoa CFC directors and players and began preparing in earnest for the forthcoming season. The existing squad needed to regain their fitness, new players would have to be signed and those that could no longer perform to the levels Garbutt demanded would have to move on to lesser teams.

Garbutt launched himself into his work, relieved to be on the training pitch once more after witnessing trench warfare at first hand. He put his contacts to work and a 'friendly' game was arranged against a team of British professionals serving in the forces. The game, played on 20 April 1919, ended in an unremarkable goalless draw. Despite this, the date has gone down in Genoa CFC history due to the fact that it was the day Genoa legend Ottavio Barbieri made his debut for his home-town club as a nineteen-year-old.

As well as being tactically astute, Garbutt had an eye for ability in young players and it was while watching the game preceding Genoa's that his eye had been caught by a young midfielder. Being a man down, Garbutt went into the dressing room at the end of the game and asked the youngster if he would like to turn out for Genoa.

Realising that a dream opportunity like this might never come his way again, Barbieri grabbed his chance and played his second full ninety minutes of the day, impressing the Genoa coach so much that he was signed by the club. Barbieri went on to appear for Genoa on 299 occasions between 1919–32 (his only club as a player) and had two spells as coach between 1939–1941 and 1945–46.

Genoa progressed through the regional qualifying group with ease, amassing forty-nine goals in only ten games. Such was their dominance that they were considered as early favourites for the title. They duly reached the northern regional final, to be contested along with Juventus and Internazionale in a round-robin tournament.

In the game against Juventus at a neutral venue in Milan, Santamaria gave Genoa an early lead. A series of questionable decisions made by the referee Varisco turned the game, and arguably the destination of the title, on its head. The first of these came when Varisco awarded Juventus a highly disputed penalty after half an hour.

Only minutes later Varisco again enraged Garbutt and his Genoa players by allowing a goal to Juventus, ignoring Genoa's claims of a blatant offside. Such was the sense of injustice among Garbutt's men that two of them were sent off following the lengthy protests that followed. These included a once-in-a-career dismissal for the man recognised as the ultimate professional and 'gentleman' – captain Renzo De Vecchi. Team-mate Della Casa was also expelled and Traverso walked from the field voluntarily. Amazingly, Genoa played on with only eight players. Despite the valiant effort made by the eight, they narrowly lost 3-2.

The game, however, has gone down in history as one in a long list of those that were ultimately decided more on the whim of the referee in charge or political machinations behind the scenes than a true reflection of the games' actual events.

Internazionale duly went on to win the title that season, their second, by beating Livorno 3-2 in the national final held in Bologna in June 1920.

The following season of 1920–21 was a frustrating one for Garbutt and his team. It would not prove to be entirely fruitless, however, for during the regional qualifying games against local side SPES Genova, the Genoa manager again made a mental note of an opposition goalkeeper, Giovanni De Prà. One might conclude that with his shock of dark hair piled high above his head, he was rather difficult to miss.

Garbutt ensured that De Prà signed for his side at the season's end and a Genoa legend was born. Born in Genova in 1900, the goalkeeper would go on to make 304 appearances for *rossoblu* from 1921–30, representing the national team nineteen times. It was while playing in one of these games, against Spain in Milan on 9 March 1924, that De Prà fractured his arm. Amazingly, he played on with the injury and helped his team to a share of the spoils in a goalless draw.

Genoa reached the final of the northern league in the 1921–22 season and when they gained a goalless draw away to Pro Vercelli on 7 May 7 1922 they must have thought that the hard work had been done. Just a week later their hopes were dashed when Pro Vercelli beat them 2-1 at the Marassi. It was to be another case of 'so near, yet so far'.

Despite the disappointments, Garbutt was not downcast for long. He was slowly but surely building a side that was soon to achieve something that never had been before and would not be repeated for many years.

Away from the football field, Italian society continued to spiral out of control. Politically, the country was hopelessly polarised. A poorly organised general strike was called by the socialists in early August 1922. Within days, black-shirted thuggery and intimidation had broken the strike and Mussolini and his fascists were suddenly seen by the middle classes and industrialists as upholders of law and order.

William Garbutt's views on the political situation surrounding him remain unknown. No correspondence exists to give any clue as to his opinion of Mussolini's fascists. In some respects he might be seen as a natural supporter of the fascists; his income would certainly include him in the middle-class bracket and it is very unlikely that he held any extreme left-wing sympathies. On the other hand, only four years earlier he had made his way home from the Western front where he had played his own small part in ensuring Europe remained free from tyranny.

Even an optimist such as Garbutt undoubtedly was could not have foretold of the success that the 1922–23 season would bring following Genoa's 4-1 defeat of Milan in the first game of the campaign on 8 October 1922. The Englishman had created a powerful Genoa side, built on the dual strengths of a resilient defence and a potent attack. Genoa duly won the next two games by the same 2-1 scoreline, away to Cremonese and on 22 October at home to Bologna.

Just days later, fascist squads occupied telephone exchanges and railway stations in the north of the country. The insurrection had begun. The Italian monarch, King Vittorio Emmanuel, backtracked on his decision to crush the uprising and in the ensuing power vacuum, invited Mussolini to become the prime minister of Italy on 29 October 1922.

Vittorio Pozzo recognised the great ability in the Genoa side and chose five of them to represent the *Azzurri* in the national team's friendly match against Germany in Milan on New Year's Day, 1923. Barbieri, Bergamino, Burlando, Santamaria and De Vecchi helped Italy to a 3-1 victory. Meanwhile, Genoa, with De Prà in goal, along with the sublime De Vecchi and Barbieri, conceded a miserly eighteen goals in twenty-one regional qualifying games. At the other end of the field, Garbutt had added the attacking prowess of Catto to that of regulars Santamaria and Sardi.

In the same twenty-one qualifying games, Genoa amassed a total of fifty-nine goals. The side remained unbeaten during this period and would go forward to the regional semi-finals where they would compete against old rivals Pro Vercelli, and Padova.

The first of these semi-finals was played away to Pro Vercelli on 13 May, the game ending in stalemate. Almost a month passed before the next game, in which Genoa trounced Padova 3-1 at the Marassi. On the 24 June, Genoa, again at home, defeated Pro Vercelli by a single goal. The semi-finals were duly wrapped up with a comfortable 3-0 win at Padova.

Genoa would seek their eighth title by playing a two-legged final against Lazio of Rome. The tie was effectively decided after the first leg played on 15 July 1923 when Genoa crushed the Romans 4-1 with Catto, Mariani, Barbieri and Santamari (penalty) scoring. The Genovese public were exuberant. Their optimism was justified, for when they travelled to the Italian capital a week later Genoa completed the execution of Lazio by again winning, this time by 2-0 with further goals from Catto and Santamaria.

Prior to the victory, Garbutt and his players were treated to an audience with Pope Pius XI and Mussolini. In winning the title, Genoa had managed something remarkable: they had remained unbeaten throughout an entire season, a feat never before achieved and not to be repeated for almost seventy years. Along with Spensley, Ferraris, De Vecchi, Barbieri and De Prà, William Garbutt would be accorded legendary status by the Genoa *tifosi* as the creator and leader of this Genoa side.

Following their title win, Genoa were a team in demand. Club officials accepted an invitation to tour South America and play against Argentinean and Uruguayan opposition, one more example of how forward thinking Genoa were at this time in comparison with the founders of the game. The accusation of being innovative is not one that could be levelled at the Football Association without some effort.

And so, only six days after victory against Lazio in Rome had earned Genoa Cricket & Football Club the title of champions of Italy, William Garbutt, club officials and a squad of seventeen players were given a hero's farewell by the *rossoblu tifosi* as they set sail from Genova on 28 July 1923, bound for South America. Climbing the gang-plank in Genova to board the *Principessa Mafalda*, these pioneers had a gruelling seventeen-day journey ahead, with brief stop-overs, including at Barcelona, San Vicente in the Cape Verde Islands, Rio de Janeiro, Santos and Montivideo.

The journey would replicate that made by thousands upon thousands of Italians before them: South America, and particularly Argentina, had become a favoured destination for many of those seeking their fortune in a new land. Indeed, many Genovese had headed for the *La Boca* quarter of Buenos Aires and settled to make it their home. Boca Juniors, the local football team, had been founded by five young Italian immigrants and the club's nickname, *Xeneizes* (Zeneizes in Genovese) is taken from Zena, being the name for Genova in Genovese dialect.

The long journey over, Genoa played their first competitive game on Argentinian soil at the Barracas Stadium in Buenos Aires on 19 August against Combinado Norte, an all-star team representing those playing for teams based in the north of the city. The official trip had raised a great deal of interest, not least among the Italian expatriate community. The winner of the game was to receive a trophy donated by the local Italian language newspaper *Giornale d'Italia*. No doubt this particular journal had hoped that the winner would be Genoa, but this was not to be; despite taking the lead through an own goal, the Italians eventually lost 2-1. Though perhaps lacking somewhat in the magnanimity required on these occasions, Genoa's captain, De Vecchi, blamed the defeat on exhaustion following the tiring journey.

The second game was also contested in Buenos Aires, this time against a *Combinado Sud* team on 2 September. At the end of this game, the team and the Genovese in the crowd went away happy following a 1-0 win following a goal by the prolific Edoardo Catto. A hurried journey to Montivideo, capital of Uruguay, followed for Garbutt and his men where they were scheduled to meet the Uruguayan national team on 5 September.

Again for this game, a trophy was donated, this time by the *Banco Italiano del Uruguay*. Individuals and companies alike were eager to have their name connected in some way with the tour. For this game, all the players were presented with gold medals donated by a group of local Italian war veterans and the Italian Ambassador gave himself the honour of taking the kick-off. Genoa, though losing 2-1, were not disgraced.

One of the Uruguayans who scored that day, Héctor Scaróne, would go on to become his nation's all-time leading goalscorer with thirty-one goals from only fifty-one games and was part of the Uruguayan team which won the gold medal at the 1924 and 1928 Olympic football tournaments and took the inaugural Jules Rimet Trophy in 1930.

A hasty return to Buenos Aires followed where the tour finale was to be played on 9 September against the Argentinian national side. Once again the game could not be played out without due ceremony, on this occasion the match-ball being delivered to the stadium by aeroplane! Fittingly perhaps, honours were even at the end of the game which ended 1-1.

The tour was a great financial and diplomatic success for Genoa, with games contested in front of large, enthusiastic crowds.

Though undeniably exhausting, the tour was also a personal success for Garbutt. A keen observer of the game and despite the comparative inexperience of the opposition, the Genoa coach always felt that he could learn something new, whether with regard to team formations or tactics or in taking the opportunity to look first hand at South American footballers he thought might make an impact in the Italian game.

The trip to South America had enabled him to do this well in advance of any of the other European coaches. The tour also strengthened the great bond between Garbutt and his players, the benefits of which would be seen once more during the forthcoming season.

Following his return from South America, William enjoyed a short break with Anna and Stuart. Having won two Italian championships, his stock as a coach was at an all-time high. Despite this, his exploits continued to fail to grab the attention of the British press. The lack of recognition does not appear to have caused him any undue concern; he seems to have been content in the knowledge that he was doing a fine job for Genoa.

Still, he must have yearned to pit his managerial wits against the finest coaches 'back home' and one wonders if any English club ever approached him in an effort to replicate the success he enjoyed with Genoa.

Even while Garbutt and the Genoa team were departing for their South American tour, events were taking place in Italy that would continue to have a profound effect for many years to come. In July of 1923, Mussolini introduced a bill in parliament which proposed that if a party secured one quarter of the vote, it would receive two-thirds of the seats in the chamber. Such an arrangement would, Mussolini argued, rid Italy of its reliance upon the weak coalition governments that had plagued the country for years. Thanks in part to this ballot rigging and the general air of intimidation created by the hired blackshirts, the general election held in April 1924 saw the fascists (in an electoral pact with the right wing of the Liberal Party) secure sixty-six per cent of the vote, thereby increasing the number of Fascist deputies in the chamber ten-fold from only thirty-five to three hundred and seventy-four.

Garbutt and his Genoa side began the defence of their title with a home fixture against Casale on 7 October 1923. When they smashed six goals past their hapless opposition it appeared that this season was but a continuation of the previous one, with the points tally growing ever higher game by game. Included in the run of success was a game in Milan against Internazionale at the end of October. Genoa were leading the match 2-1 with only minutes remaining when play was suspended following a pitch invasion. In such cases, the football federation awarded the points from the match to the 'wronged' team; in this particular instance, Genoa being awarded a 2-0 *a tavolino* win. On 11 November, Genoa's unbeaten run finally ended when they lost by three goals to one in an away match against Livorno. This was the first occasion, aside from the South American tour, that Garbutt's side has lost a game since 14 May 1921, thirty months earlier!

Perhaps predictably, Genoa found it impossible to repeat the amazing success of the previous season. Nevertheless, they were still far and away the strongest team in the group and topped the regional league when the last match was played on 13 April. In finishing top with thirty-three points, Genoa had finished four points clear of their nearest rival Padova, winning fourteen matches, drawing five and losing three. In scoring fifty goals and conceding only thirteen, they had been stronger both in attack and defence than any of their opponents. As title holders, and in a strong position in the 1923–24 season, Genoa held a prominent position in Italian football.

William Garbutt was a proud man when Vittorio Pozzo, coach of the *Azzurri,* named six Genoa players in the Italian team to face Spain in a friendly played in front of twenty thousand in Milan on 9 March 1924. Garbutt's six men were De Prà, De Vecchi, Barbieri, Burlando, Leale and Catto. Another indication of the high regard Pozzo held for Garbutt can be seen by the Italian coach asking the Englishman to assist him in preparing the *Azzurri* for the Olympic football tournament to be held in Paris in 1924. Lanfranchi has gone so far as to suggest that Garbutt acted as a co-manager to the team.[33]

Whatever role he played, Garbutt was extremely honoured to accept Pozzo's request, and set about the task with gusto. In the game immediately preceding the tournament, Hungary had demolished the Italians 7-1 in a friendly in Budapest. It was blatantly obvious to Pozzo that the defence needed an urgent overhaul and, with four Genoa defenders in the squad, Garbutt's rapport with his players was seen as crucial. Pozzo also recruited another Englishman, Herbert Burgess, to complete the triumvirate. Burgess had played at left-back for both Manchester clubs and been capped by England before a knee injury ended his playing career in 1910, prompting him, like Garbutt, to seek a coaching post on the continent.

Clearly, the decision to appoint two Englishman to assist in the preparations would not have been popular with the nationalists within the top echelons of Italian football but Pozzo held firm. Football had gone from being a demonstration sport at the first Olympic Games to the de-facto World Championship during the 1920s, losing this pre-eminence when the Jules Rimet trophy was contested in 1930.

The Italians' opening fixture in the Games was against Spain on 25 May 1924 with a late own goal by Vallana giving the *Azzurri* all the points. Pozzo saw the clean sheet as a vindication of his decision to appoint Garbutt. This view would have been strengthened when, in the second game played four days later, Italy, with goals from Baloncieri and Della Valle, beat Luxembourg 2-0. In the quarter-finals held on 2 June, Italy was drawn against Switzerland. The first forty-five minutes remained cagey with neither side able to force an advantage. In the second half, however, the Swiss scored twice to Italy's one, thus ending the Italians' involvement in the tournament. It had been another valuable learning experience for Garbutt and he was held in high regard by the Italian national coach ever after. Following Italy's elimination from the Games, only two weeks remained until Genoa were due to play Bologna in the first of the two-legged final encounters to decide which team would dispute the regional final. Garbutt was desperately keen to ensure that none of the Genoa players representing the *Azzurri* picked up injuries before these key games. As it was, De Prá, Barbieri, Burlando and De Vecchi all returned to Italy relatively unscathed.

Just days before the Genoa–Bologna clash, Italy was plunged into its latest political crisis. Giacomo Matteotti, the socialist deputy, had long been an outspoken critic of fascist intimidation and oppression. In a speech to parliament on 30 May 1924 (that was interrupted 'a hundred times')[34] Matteotti denounced Mussolini and the tactics employed by his followers. On 10 June, the brave Matteotti was kidnapped, stabbed to death and later found buried in the Roman countryside. For a period, the public revulsion at the murder was such that Mussolini's regime appeared to be on the very brink of collapse.

Upon qualifying from the regional group, Genoa would face Bologna in the northern regional finals in Genova on 15 June. Garbutt faced his men in the home dressing room before the game, ensuring they focussed on the task ahead.

Small details were addressed, nothing considered too insignificant to receive attention. The fact that both sides knew each other so well meant that the game was reduced to something of a stalemate and appeared to be heading for a goalless draw when Neri pounced only minutes from the end to give Genoa a crucial advantage. A week later, Genoa travelled to Bologna for the second leg where they would defend their slender lead in front of a passionate home crowd determined to play a part in securing the victory that would see Bologna reach the final.

As was the case in the first leg a week before, the game was a tense affair; neither side appeared prepared to take the risk that might prise open the other. The onus was on Bologna to score with Genoa doing what they did so well. Defensively they were among the strongest sides in Italy. When a breakthrough did come, it came with a goal from Santamaria after thirty-six minutes. What an excellent servant Santamaria had been for Genoa and his *Mister*. The goal gave Genoa a two-goal advantage, one that Bologna would find difficult to overcome.

The home supporters' hopes were raised momentarily after fifty-seven minutes when Pozzi scored for Bologna from the penalty spot. The tension in the stadium built to an almost unbearable level and Garbutt needed to draw upon all his experience as a player and coach to see his side through the remaining thirty-three minutes.

When it became apparent to the Bologna supporters that their team was not going to overhaul Genoa's

2-1 lead, a riot ensued and a pitch invasion resulted in the referee abandoning the contest two minutes from the end of the game. Once again, the federation awarded the unfinished game 2-0 to Genoa.

The rivals would meet each other at the same stage in the following season with a similar controversial outcome but then it would be fascists that would ultimately decide the outcome of the game and not the football federation. For now though, Garbutt and his team celebrated reaching the championship final.

This time Savoia, a team based near Naples, would provide the opposition, again a two-legged affair. At the end of August, Genoa hosted the first leg. In front of an expectant crowd they mounted attack after attack upon the Savoia goal. After fifteen minutes of unrelenting pressure, their efforts were rewarded when Catto opened the scoring. Genoa were on their way.

The lead was doubled in the very next attack, this time Sardi slotting home. Garbutt's half-time talk was spent demanding they concentrate on the task ahead, not to be complacent or get carried away. Soon after the restart, Savoia fought their way back into the game when Bobbio scored after forty-nine minutes. Garbutt's anxiety was relieved, however, when Santamaria restored the two-goal lead with fifty-five minutes played. The remainder of the game was played out without further incident and Genoa took their two-goal advantage into the game to be played a week later on 7 September 1924.

This was tighter and somewhat an anti-climax, which ended in an honourable draw and a 4-2 aggregate win for Genoa. Genoa's retention of their championship was the ninth occasion they had been crowned champions of Italy and came exactly thirty-one years after being founded. It was William Garbutt's third title and cemented his Midas-like reputation with the followers of the Ligurians.

Though now at the peak of his coaching career, once again it appears that the achievement was seen as unworthy of mention in the English newspapers. As a special award, the Italian federation had decided to introduce a tricolor badge to be worn on the jerseys of the championship-winning side, an award Genoa wore with pride. Largely through events that were to transpire the following season, this has proved to be the very last occasion the badge has adorned the shirts of the *rossoblu*.

Chapter 5
The Bologna Scandal

The 1924–25 season was one of the most dramatic and infamous in the history of the youthful Italian football league. It was played out against a backdrop of increasing attacks on freedom in all areas of Italian life as the fascists established their dictatorship by systematically suffocating the press and effectively banning opposition parties by introducing a law on association.

In an act of bravado, Mussolini, perhaps aware that he had the active support of the King and the tacit support of the Vatican, had stood up before the Italian Parliament and accepted total responsibility for the murder of Giacomo Matteotti, and challenged the chamber to do as it saw fit. In its failure to respond, Procacci claims that:

> *the chamber signed its own death warrant, and the liberal state finally ceased to exist.*[35]

The Genoa line-up showed changes from that of previous seasons. One familiar name missing was that of one of Garbutt's first signings for the club, Enrico Sardi. Sardi had won three championships with Genoa, earned caps for his country and had generally proved a tremendous servant. As is the case with even the finest players, however, time had caught up with Sardi. Recognising this, Garbutt wasted no time in his search for a capable replacement.

This came in the guise of Cesare Alberti, a forward discarded by Bologna after he had suffered a serious knee injury. After becoming the first footballer in Italy to undergo an operation to his meniscus, Alberti was given the opportunity to resume his career in football at the highest level with Genoa: perhaps Garbutt recalled how his own playing career had been cruelly cut short by a similar injury when gambling on the young man's fitness and offering him a contract.

Genoa, as was the case in previous seasons, qualified from their northern regional qualifying group. On this occasion though, they had only claimed the top spot by the narrowest of margins, victory in their last game enabling them to pip Modena by a solitary point. In finishing top of their group, Bologna guaranteed that the right to play in the national final would again be contested against Genoa.

The rivalry between the two was palpable after the events of the previous season. And so, a series of games that have gone down in infamy in Italian football history began in Bologna on 24 May 1925. In this, the first leg, Genoa defeated Bologna 2-1 in their own stadium. Perhaps it was destined that

Alberti should score a goal against the side that had cast him aside at the beginning of the season. After Catto had doubled Genoa's lead with only minutes remaining, Garbutt's men must have thought they were well and truly on their way to a tenth title. If this was the case they were to be mistaken, for Bologna's clinical striker Schiavio gained his side a foothold in the tie by reducing the deficit almost on the stroke of full-time.

Still, with a goal advantage and the second leg to be played in Genova a week later, Garbutt and his players remained confident. This was tested when Bologna scored through Muzzioli in the first half. Santamaria restored Genoa's advantage when he scored after seventy-three minutes which left seventeen minutes for them to hold on to a lead that would see them through to the national final against opposition they were sure they would overcome easily.

Disaster struck when Giuseppe Della Valle thrust a dagger into the heart of Genoa by bringing parity to the game on eighty-three minutes. The contrast between the two sets of supporters was stark, the home contingent stunned into silence whereas the five hundred or so Bologna *tifosi* erupted. The two sides would need to play another game to find a winner. It was decided that this was to be played at a neutral venue, Milan, on 7 June.

Garbutt was concerned that his defensive rock, Barbieri, would not be available for the game, probably because of injury. Such an influential player was bound to be missed.

Garbutt's fears appeared to be unfounded when Genoa struck the first blow, Daniele Moruzzi scoring after only twelve minutes. The lead was extended when Alberti again relished the delight of scoring against his former club. With Genoa two goals to the good against Bologna, surely a berth in the final was theirs? Then came the incident which still stains the history of Italian football. With half an hour remaining, a Muzzioli shot towards the Genoa goal was pushed athletically around the post by Genoa's goalkeeper De Prá. The match referee, Giovanni Mauro, immediately whistled for a corner kick.

On this the Bologna players surrounded the official and many of their supporters, led by fascist blackshirts, invaded the pitch, insisting the ball had entered the net and their team be awarded a goal. One of these supporters was Leandro Arpinati, a forty-three-year-old fascist and friend of Mussolini, who had taken part in the march on Rome and would go on to become the President of the Italian Football Federation (FIGC). As Under Secretary of the Interior, Arpinati was known as the 'Second Duce of Fascism'.[36]

The referee was surrounded by arguing, jostling players for almost fifteen minutes and, mindful of the threat posed by supporters on the field of play, went back on his original decision and awarded a goal to the visitors. In truth, Mauro had collapsed under the sheer weight of intimidation placed upon him by Arpinati and his Bolognese fascists. Garbutt stood watching the events unfolding in disbelief.

Genoa's captain, De Vecchi questioned Mauro and received an assurance that the goal had only been given to ensure public safety. Furthermore, Mauro indicated that Genoa would be awarded another *a tavolino* win as in the corresponding game the season before, as per the league's regulations where a pitch invasion had occurred. After eighty-two minutes, Pozzi 'equalised' for Bologna. Garbutt refused to allow his Genoa team to entertain any farcical notion of extra time.

Perhaps somewhat naively, given the social and political situation prevailing in Italy at the time, the Genoa players walked from the pitch confident that the federation would rise above politics, show courage and make a just decision by punishing Bologna for the pitch invasion that had marred the match.

Garbutt listened in disbelief as he was told of the FIGC's decision to order yet another re-match. How could the invasion be so blatantly ignored? Quite simply, Mauro's post-match report reduced the 'pitch invasion' to a description of the presence of some supporters on the pitch. The difference in emphasis was enough to ensure Genoa were not awarded the game as they had been led to expect and were required to play against Bologna once more.

Another explanation for the bizarre decision by the FIGC to order another match might be explained by the parlous state of the organisation's finances. The five-game epic between these two giants of Italian football swelled the coffers of the FIGC and possibly saved it from bankruptcy.

And so, in Turin on 5 July 1925, William Garbutt again attempted to raise the spirits of his Genoa players, imploring them to put behind them the injustice to which they had been subjected in Milan a month earlier and go on and win the tie.

This game, unlike the previous one, passed without great incident, Schiavio opened the scoring for Bologna after only eleven minutes, a lead which Catto cancelled after twenty-five minutes. No further goals were added by either side despite playing extra time and so, remarkably, another game would be required to seek a winner.

It was events following the game in Turin that caused controversy on this occasion. As supporters of both teams gathered in Turin's Porta Nuova station waiting to board trains to their respective cities, fights broke out. Dramatically, pistol shots rang out from a train carrying Bologna supporters resulting in injury to two Genoa rivals.

After Genoa had been advised by the FIGC that any re-match against Bologna was unlikely to take place before September, Garbutt made the most of the opportunity and took Anna and Stuart away for a much-needed break. The whole episode had been exhausting for him, both mentally and physically.

Similarly, the Genoa squad headed for the quiet and solitude of the mountains. On 8 August, however, almost a month after the game in Turin, the Genoa club was informed by the FIGC that they were to play the game against Bologna in Milan on the following day, behind closed doors and at 7am in the morning! Had Genoa refused to play, as they must surely have been tempted, it was made clear to them that they could have been wound up as a club.

Turin had again been asked to stage the match, a request the city's authorities declined on account of the earlier disorder. And so, Genoa's coach, players and officials rushed back to the city to make their way to the neutral venue in Milan that would host the match.

The game kicked off in an eerie atmosphere. The players were not used to playing in such conditions, the only noise the sound of their own voices. It soon became apparent that, unlike their Bolognese opponents, the Genoa team lacked match fitness.

Bologna had, it transpired, continued training and preparing for the game, seemingly advised well in advance when the game would be played. A goal after twenty-eight minutes gave Bologna the lead and despite Garbutt's half-time exhortations his players had given all they had to give. Their lack of fitness proved crucial and Perin added the *coup de grâce* just before the end of the contest. Bologna had won the latest battle in the epic war between the two sides 2-1.

Garbutt's men trudged disconsolately from the field, exhausted, angry and bitter. There was little the *Mister* could say to them on this occasion that would soften the blow. Defeat would mean that Genoa at the time of writing are still marooned on nine championship titles, one short of the magical number required for an Italian team to wear the star denoting their tenth championship. Only three teams are currently able to sport the star, Juventus (with two), Internazionale and AC Milan. In the final played out over two legs in August, Bologna went on to gain their first ever championship title, beating Alba Roma at a canter, 6-0 on aggregate.

The question about who did most to ensure the title headed for Emilia-Romagna is a subject of heated debate among the *tifosi* of the Genoa and Bologna clubs to this day. Giovanni Mauro, the lawyer/referee who officiated during the fateful third game, went on to become the head of a special committee set up to oversee the modernisation of the game in Italy under the *Carta di Viareggio* of 1926. As John Foot has written, Mauro's part in the 'Bologna "theft" ... had done his career no harm at all.'[37]

Leandro Arpinati fared less well in the long term. Despite attaining the prominent position of Under Secretary of the Interior, a post he held from 1929 to May 1934, Arpinati had attracted enemies within his own party. In his position as Bologna's mayor and leading fascist, Arpinati invited Mussolini to the city to celebrate the opening of its new Littoriale stadium. When *il Duce* was being chauffeured in an open-top car, an assassination attempt was made on his life.

A sixteen-year-old youth, Anteo Zamboni, was made a scapegoat and lynched by fascists, his young body mercilessly stabbed and battered by the angry mob. Achille Starace, the secretary of the Fascist Party, always suspected Arpinati of involvement in the assassination attempt on the basis that he was a close friend of the Zamboni family. Arrested

A young William (front row, first left) in the colours of his first team,
Edgeley FC

A professional with Woolwich Arsenal FC 1906–07 (bottom row, second left)

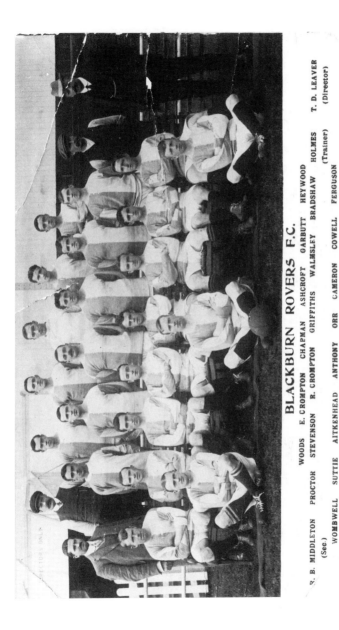

BLACKBURN ROVERS F.C.

WOODS E. CROMPTON CHAPMAN ASHCROFT GARBUTT HEYWOOD

R. B. MIDDLETON PROCTOR STEVENSON R. CROMPTON GRIFFITHS WALMSLEY BRADSHAW HOLMES T. D. LEAVER

(See.) WOMBWELL SUTTIE AITKENHEAD ANTHONY ORR CAMERON COWELL FERGUSON (Trainer) (Director)

BRACEGIRDLE DAVIES LATHERON Photo by B. Scott & Co. Manchester

Garbutt with Blackburn Rovers FC (back row, second right)

Anna Stewart, Garbutt's wife

Garbutt in uniform, with Anna and son Stuart (top)
In the uniform of the 99th Battery Royal Field Artillery (bottom)

(above) Garbutt in Genova with son Stuart in replica Genoa jersey (left) with John Wylie Grant, fellow Englishman and Genoa striker before the outbreak of World War One

RECORD 16 → 0

GENOA CLUB   GOALS 16

(top) Garbutt with Percy Walsingham and Grant
(above) Garbutt's Genoa team that demolished Acqui 16-0 on
4 October 1914 (courtesy Archivio fotografico Fondazione Genoa 1893)

Garbutt (standing far left) with the Italian national team in Berne for Friendly international against Switzerland on 17 May, 1914

Commemorative postcard of Genoa's 1914–15 championship winning team showing an early Marassi Stadium (courtesy Archivio fotografico Fondazione Genoa 1893)

Garbutt with Genoa squad in 1920 (courtesy Archivio fotografico
Fondazione Genoa 1893)

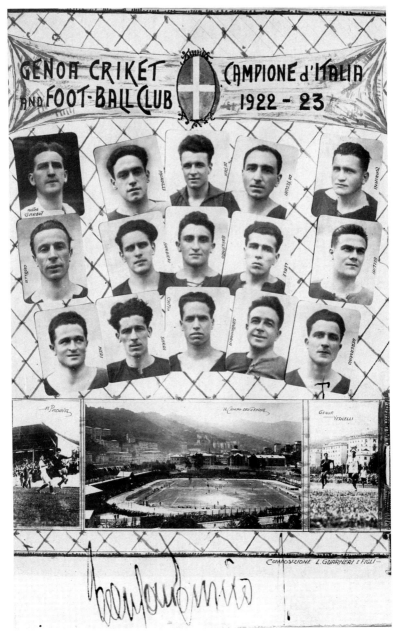

Another postcard commemorating another Genoa championship, this time the 1922–23 squad (courtesy Archivio fotografico Fondazione Genoa 1893)

Garbutt with the Italian squad for the 1924 Summer Olympic football tournament. The legendary Azzurri coach Vittorio Pozzo
stands far right

Fascist salutes at Genoa's 40th anniversary celebrations in 1933

(top) Garbutt surrounded by former players at the benefit game arranged for him by Genoa FC on June 24 1951 and (above) with ex-internationals and former Genoa players at the benefit game

Cimitero Piratello, Imola, Italy, last resting place of Anna Stewart

The unassuming terraced property in Priory Road, Warwick that was
Garbutt's last home

on 26 July 1934 on charges of plotting against Mussolini's regime and unsurprisingly found guilty at his trial, Arpinati was sentenced to be confined to a penal settlement on the island of Lipari off the north coast of Sicily from 1934–37. Following this he was confined to the village of Malacappa near to Bologna. Like many fascists, he was eventually killed by partisans upon the liberation of Italy on 22 April 1945.

Everyone connected with Genoa realised that there was little to be gained from dwelling on the injustice of the Bologna result. Recriminations would, of course, continue between the two sets of fans for many years, but the directors, Garbutt and the players accepted the need to move on. For his part, Garbutt had enough on his mind working to rebuild the side. Players were coming to the end of their careers and would need to be replaced.

Augusto Bergamino was one who hung up his boots. Another, Bellini, joined Internazionale. Garbutt bade a sad farewell to faithful Genoa servants in Ettore Leale and Santamaria. Both champions and internationals, Genoa would not see their like again. Leale had served Garbutt since 1913, in a strong midfield trio alongside Barbieri and Burlando. His left-wing partnership with De Vecchi was one of the main reasons for the success enjoyed by the *rossoblu*.

It has been suggested that he walked away from the game at this stage due to his bitterness at the outcome of the Bologna farce. Aristodemo Santamaria had also been a great servant since Garbutt had gambled on taking him and Sardi to Genoa some twelve years earlier, signings which incurred the wrath of the federation.

As a long-standing professional, Garbutt understood that all footballers had their day and that teams must rebuild. New players would be drafted in. One of these, Virgilio Levratto, had already made an impact in the Italian game and was another to play for Genoa under Garbutt who would go on to become a national legend. Garbutt had witnessed his ability at first hand when assisting Pozzo with the *Azzurri* at the Paris Olympics only the year before.

The season before joining Genoa, Levratto had starred for Hellas Verona (scoring fifteen goals from only twenty games), his powerful shot earning him the nickname 'netbreaker.' In a career with Genoa that would span 1925–32, he would go on to score eighty-four goals in 148 games for the Genovese.

Ultimately, the 1925–26 season, when compared with Genoa's recent great achievements, would go down as a dismal failure. The side finished third in their northern regional league, adrift not only of Cremonese in the runners-up place but a massive nine points behind Juventus, who went on to win the title.

Juventus enjoyed a prowess in attack the rest of the league could only envy. Hirzer scored twenty-nine goals, with Pastore adding a further twenty. Catto was Genoa's top scorer that season with thirteen goals, Levratto contributing a further eleven but it was perhaps the tragic loss to the team of Cesarino

(Cesare) Alberti that was most damaging in the long term. Alberti had died aged just twenty-one. Ill after eating infected seafood, he passed away at 4 a.m. on 14 March 1926, only hours before his team were due to play at home to Livorno. The game was a sombre affair, reflecting the mood among Alberti's former team-mates. Already that season he had scored eight goals in only eleven matches.

At the season's close, Garbutt and his directors sat down to discuss the terms of his new contract. Garbutt was reported to have been somewhat 'perplexed'[38] at the original offer, one that, without doubt, reflected the board's concerns at the lack of success. Eventually Garbutt accepted a salary of 2,500 lire per month, a package sweetened to some extent by the promise that he would receive the total gate receipts from a friendly game to be arranged.

Warning bells may have been sounding at this stage for Garbutt and he was only too aware that he would need to bring back success to Genoa in the 1926–27 season. Failing this, his stock as coach of Genoa might diminish and the terms of any future contract could well reduce accordingly.

Italy reflected the rest of the continent in that football experienced a massive explosion in popularity after the Great War. In no time at all it became Italy's national sport. The fascists were quick to realise the potential the game offered them as regards access to the masses.

Up until the creation of the *Carta di Viareggio* in 1926, the organisation of the game in Italy was the antithesis of everything the fascists represented.

Disunity between smaller and larger teams, crowd trouble, questionable refereeing standards and large numbers of foreign players and coaches in the Italian game were all issues that the *Carta* sought to resolve. The constitution officially paved the way for professionalism to be introduced, recognising that players were already paid, often by illicit, underhand means.

In seeking to promote the notion of Italian racial supremacy, foreign players were to be banned. Aware, however, that many clubs had already made future commitments to foreigners, these clubs were permitted to sign two each for the 1926–27 season, on the proviso that only one could be used during each game.

It was not only foreign players who came under attack from the *Carta di Viareggio*. Non-Italian coaches were also considered fair game. Augusto Turati, the Extraordinary Commissioner of CONI *(Comitato Olimpico Nazionale Italiano)*, held as unfavourable a view of foreign coaches as he did players. Limits on the number of foreign coaches plying their trade in the Italian game were imposed and clubs wishing to employ *stranieri* would first need to seek permission from CONI.

This all-pervading control of the game by the fascists even sought to amend its terminology, and references to the *Trainer*, or the one coined for Garbutt, *Mister*, being cited by fascists as examples of foreign degeneracy, with the Florentine sports weekly *Lo Stadio* calling for the Italian equivalent *Maestro* to be used in its place. A national league, the forerunner of the modern-day *Serie A* and *B*, would also be born out of the charter, replacing the fragmented regional leagues.

The 1926–27 campaign was a strange one for Genoa. Their season began with a home game against Brescia in which Garbutt's men triumphed 4-1. But while their home form remained good they dropped too many points away from the Marassi. In their eighteen qualifying matches, Genoa won eight of their nine home games but the *Rossoblu* were able to muster only two victories, along with four draws, and three defeats, away from home.

Despite the poor showing in the qualifying phase, Genoa still managed to join Juventus and Internazionale as the three teams from their group to proceed to the national finals. They were joined by Bologna, Milan and Torino in a round-robin tournament to decide the season's championship.

Frustratingly for Garbutt, his team's poor away form continued into the knock-out phase. At the Marassi, they gained maximum points against Bologna, Milan and Torino and earned a 1-1 draw against Internazionale. Their sole loss on home soil was a 3-2 defeat against Juventus. Away from home, however, Genoa continued to display their Jekyll and Hyde tendencies, beating only Internazionale. Defeats to Bologna (1-0), Juventus (6-0), Milan (4-2), and Torino (3-1) ensured the season would end in disappointment.

When Garbutt gave his pre-match team talk to the assembled Genoa players in the visitors' changing room before the game against Internazionale in

Milan on 3 July 1927, he must have known it was his last as Genoa coach. One can only imagine the mixed emotions he was feeling as he prepared to bid farewell to the team he had led to three Italian championships. It was time to move on, however. Having been persuaded, perhaps against his better judgement, to renew his contract the previous season, Garbutt made it clear that he would not remain in control for the one to come. Nevertheless, by assuring the directors of his confidence in his nominated replacement, he was instrumental in the appointment of one of his first signings, the 'son of God,' Renzo De Vecchi as the new *Mister* of the *Rossoblu*. The issue of his successor resolved, Garbutt was now able to move on to the next chapter of his career.

It was Torino who finished first at the end of the 1926–27 season but their success was to give rise to the next controversy to damage the Italian game. An executive of Torino, Nani, had offered a bribe of 50,000 lire to the Juventus left-back, Luigi Allemandi, to play poorly and thereby help Torino win the derby game.

Half was to be paid beforehand with the balance payable after victory had been delivered. Torino duly won 2-1 but Nani, supposedly angered by Allemandi's strong performance, refused to hand over the remaining twenty-five thousand lire. An argument between the two was overheard, in what must have been the scoop of his life, by a journalist named Fermanelli who worked for a Rome-based sports journal.

Fermanelli revealed this exclusive story of scandal and deceit to a stunned, though perhaps not entirely surprised, Italian public. Part of the *raison d'etre* for the introduction of the *Carta di Viareggio* had been to clean up *calcio* and to remove scandals such as these from the game. Arpinati and the FIGC needed to be seen to be acting decisively and Torino were duly stripped of the title. Although Bologna had finished runners-up, Arpinati knew that even he dare not present the title to the side with which he was so closely linked, and so the championship remained unallocated. Allemandi was initially banned but later received a pardon from King Umberto and would go on to win Olympic bronze for the *Azzurri* in 1928 and was part of the Italian team crowned world champions in 1934.

Chapter 6
The Road Leads to Rome

N ow in his mid-forties, Garbutt was widely respected throughout the Italian game, enjoyed
a wealth of knowledge and experience and
had three championship titles under his belt. He was
extremely marketable and his successful track record
as a coach ensured that he was much in demand.
One of the architects of the *Carta di Viareggio* had
been a prominent fascist bureaucrat by the name of
Italo Foschi.

A lean, well-groomed man who wore a *pince-
nez*, Foschi would start his day with a cigarette and
chain smoke until he closed his eyes to sleep at the
end of the day. He was aware that the only way in
which the Italian capital would be able to boast a
team capable of competing against the powerful
northern-based sides of Turin, Milan, Genoa and
more lately, Bologna, would be to merge a number
of Rome's smaller teams. Up to this point, the Italian
capital had been represented by SS Lazio, Roman
FC, SS Alba-Audace Roma and Fortitudo-Pro Roma,
and even these teams had been the products of
previous mergers. The divisions, traditionally based

on neighbourhood and class lines, ensured that the teams remained weak financially and the support they enjoyed was diluted. And so, in June 1927, and with the tacit approval of the fascists, the above teams (with the notable exception of SS Lazio) combined to create a new force. Three sides, with three distinct histories and fan bases, three presidents, squads of players and coaches combined to form *Associazione Sportiva (AS) Roma.*

As the first president of the new organisation, Foschi was keen to ensure that the new team had the best possible man at the helm. Garbutt was approached and duly accepted the offer to become AS Roma's first coach. The challenge of forging a new, single identity from three disparate forces was formidable but one which Garbutt accepted enthusiastically. The first AS Roma team (with the exception of Yugoslav striker Mario Bussich, signed from Triestina) was a product of the pick of the Roman sides dismantled to create the new one.

Only a few names stand out: Cesare Fasanelli was a midfielder who would go on to make 167 appearances for AS Roma, scoring fifty-six goals while Chini Ludueña, an Argentine attacker, was AS Roma's first foreign player. Perhaps most famous of all in Garbutt's first team was Attilo Ferraris IV (so named because he was the youngest of four brothers). Ferraris is said to have preferred women to training, and displayed a fondness for alcohol and cigarettes. Nevertheless, he went on to play a vital role in Pozzo's victorious 1934 World Cup team. Given the fact that Garbutt was unable to make any significant additions to the squad, it is perhaps not surprising that the 1927–28 inaugural season turned out to be a modest one for AS Roma.

A promising start (they were joint top after the first three games) could not be maintained and Garbutt's side finished eighth out of eleven, gaining eighteen points from twenty games. The *Mister* made note of Roma's lack of a proven goalscorer, something his Genoa teams had always enjoyed. Bussich top-scored for the Romans with eight while Chini Ludueña weighed in with a further seven. In fact, the team scored only thirty-one goals.

From April 1928 onwards, Garbutt began preparing his side for its *Coppa CONI* campaign, a forerunner of the present-day *Coppa Italia*. Roma were to compete against six others: Napoli, La Dominante di Genova, Cremonese, Pro Patria, Novara and Brescia on a home and away basis. The best placed of the seven would qualify for a two-legged final against the winner of another pool of seven teams. Garbutt's team performed well in their qualifying games, winning eight, drawing two and suffering just two defeats. Only Modena would stand between Garbutt's Roma and a trophy in his first season as coach. On 22 July 1928, the two sides played out a disappointing goalless draw in front of the expectant Roman *tifosi*.

Days later, a 2-2 draw in the reverse tie at Modena meant that a play-off at a neutral venue would be necessary. Florence was chosen to host the game and on 29 July, both teams took to the field once again. Halfway through the first half, Corbyons gave Roma the lead from a penalty. Manzoni equalised for Modena and the game went into extra time. Five minutes into the second period, Bussich scored what would prove to be the winning goal.

When the news was heard by Roma's supporters crowding around the nearest available radio in the capital, the streets of the ancient capital exploded in a joyous celebration.

The cup triumph gave Garbutt immense satisfaction. His skill as a team builder and motivator of men had been instrumental in bonding a group of men, some of whom had never played with each other before, and turning them into an effective unit. The same abilities that had seen him lead Genoa to three titles and made him Italo Foschi's number one choice for the position as the first ever coach of AS Roma, had served him well again.

But all was not well at Genoa. As a more than interested bystander, Garbutt looked on at events with a confused mix of emotions – anger, sadness and concern. The fascists had made it clear that Genoa Cricket & Football Club was no longer a suitable name for a team of true Italian patriots. Henceforth, the team name would *Genova 1893*. A similar fate befell Internazionale who were forced to take on the new identity of Ambrosiana.

Once his task of creating a new Roman team finally equipped to compete against the northern sides was accomplished, Foschi moved on to a new personal challenge as Prefect for the La Spezia region in the Italian parliament. The reins of the AS Roma presidency were handed to Renato Sacerdoti in time for Garbutt's second season. Roma's weakness in front of goal was a priority for Garbutt and one he sought to address by purchasing Rodolfo Volk from Fiumana. In addition, the prodigal son, Fulvio Bernardini, was signed from Internazionale. Bernardini was born in Rome and played for Lazio before joining Internazionale (against his father's death-bed wish) before being signed by Garbutt. Still, early on in the 1928–29 season AS Roma experienced great success, as Garbutt expertly moulded the power and scoring prowess of Volk to the intelligent play of Bernardini and the artistry of Attilo Ferraris. The *giallorossi* finished the season in a lofty third place on forty points with Torino topping the group on forty-eight points and Milan runners-up on forty-two. The goal-scoring drought of the previous season had been more than adequately addressed as Volk netted twenty-four times. Chini Ludueña and Fasanelli also made useful contributions. The ability of Garbutt's side cannot be denied; in their penultimate game of the season they defeated the eventual champions Torino 6-1, Volk scoring five times.

Roma's away game to Alessandria on 17 March 1929 highlighted the fact that crowd disorder at Italian football matches had not disappeared. Home supporters, angry at seeing their heroes losing 2-0 to AS Roma, invaded the field. Roma's players fled the stadium in fear of their lives. The referee, Scarpi di Dolo, and Bernardini received serious injuries. William Garbutt meanwhile gained some measure of safety courtesy of Alessandria's directors.

At the end of his second season with AS Roma, Garbutt decided to leave. It was a perfectly amicable separation. His two campaigns with the Romans had been a success. A trophy delivered in their inaugural season, Garbutt had created a strong, competitive squad in a remarkably short period of time and guaranteed AS Roma's place in the new *Serie A* league that was to commence the following season. His professional standing in the game restored after the relative decline towards the end of his reign at Genoa, it was time for the *Mister* to continue his odyssey in what was then *Serie A's* most southerly outpost.

Chapter 7
Further South

Naples Foot-Ball & Cricket Club, as the name suggests, owed it's origins to an Englishman. William Poths worked for the Cunard Shipping Line and it was he, along with an Italian friend Ernesto Bruschini, who founded the team in 1904. The team's first competitive cricket match was probably against a team of British sailors from the ship *Arabik* who found themselves in port and looking for a spot of healthy exercise. So bewildering must the average Neapolitan have found the laws of England's summer pastime that all reference to cricket had been dropped by 1906.

In 1912, frustrated by the lack of footballing activity, a breakaway team by the name of *Unione Sportiva Internazionale Napoli* was formed. A decade would pass before the two factions would re-unite once again and take on the rather confusing Anglo-Italian title of *Foot-Ball Club Internazionale Naples* or *FBC Internaples*. Changes of teams' names must have been fashionable, for they again changed their name (and constitution) on 1 August 1926, becoming *Associazione Calcio Napoli*.

The 1926–27 season was such a disastrous one for the team that it is a wonder they ever recovered. From eighteen games contested in the regional qualifying group, the end of season statistics makes dismal reading: played eighteen, won nil, drew one, lost seventeen, goals for seven, goals against sixty-one. Red-faced and wounded, the club were relegated needless to say but then re-admitted.

They fared somewhat better in 1927–28, finishing ninth out of eleven and by ending the 1928–29 season eighth out of sixteen they guaranteed their place in the inaugural *Serie A* season of 1929–30. As had been the case when Italo Foschi was on the lookout for an experienced coach to take control of AS Roma's first-ever season, Napoli's President Giorgio Ascarelli had no hesitation in approaching the Englishman Garbutt.

For his part, Garbutt was keen to commit himself and his family to a new life with Napoli. The terms of the contract offered to him were agreeable and he welcomed the challenge of creating a team of which the passionate Neapolitans could be proud. Anna may have missed some of the elegance of Rome, but aware of the demands of her husband's occupation she gave her usual wholehearted support.

The locals welcomed the English *Mister* enthusiastically, seeing in him someone who could replicate the success he had brought to Genoa and Roma and help Napoli compete with the north. Although neither of the teams he had led had met Napoli in a competitive fixture, as a true professional Garbutt knew the strengths and weaknesses of the team he was inheriting. Giuseppe Cavanna was a talented goalkeeper who played for Napoli during Garbutt's entire reign as coach and was Pozzo's reserve 'keeper for the 1934 World Cup squad.

The legendary Antonio Vojak was the latest of the prolific goalscorers that Garbutt's teams always seemed to include. As with Cavanna, Vojak's Napoli career would also coincide with that of Garbutt and his 102 goals were scored at the rate of just over one every other game.

Due to the influence of the fascists, it was not only football teams that were required to change names that were deemed politically inappropriate: Vojak was 'influenced' to adopt 'Vogliani' as his family name.

Attila Sallustro was another player accorded legendary status by an adoring Neapolitan public. Born in Paraguay to wealthy Italian parents, when Sallustro famously refused payment to play for Napoli, the club rewarded him with a Fiat Balilla luxury car for his efforts. An effective strike partner for Vojak, Sallustro would contribute 107 goals in 259 games for Napoli. So, Garbutt recognised that his task was to once again mould a group of talented footballers into an effective unit. Fitness levels would need to be raised to cope with the physical rigours of the style of play that Garbutt required from his teams.

Garbutt's first game in charge of Napoli, and the first in the new *Serie A*, was a daunting prospect. On 6 October 1929, following a four-hundred-mile journey to the northern stronghold of Turin, Napoli would play against a strong Juventus side. After only ten minutes of this opening match, Garbutt's men were a goal down after their defender Zoccoli put through his own net. But any Juventus *tifosi* expecting an easy win for their heroes were shocked when Marcello Mihalic restored parity shortly before half-time. Garbutt's talk to his players at the interval worked well, as Napoli tore into their hosts after the restart, Mihalic silencing the home crowd with his second goal ten minutes into the second half.

Garbutt's players had expended so much effort that it was inevitable they would begin to wilt, and Juventus equalised. Mihalic capped an eventful game for himself by being sent off. Only four minutes from the end of the game, a heroic draw for the ten remaining Napoli players was snatched away when Munerati scored for Juventus.

Another fixture that Garbutt had circled on his calendar was 10 November 1929. Six games into the season, Garbutt faced one of his former teams for the first time in a truly competitive game when Napoli played at AS Roma's legendary Testaccio stadium. On this occasion, Napoli left with a very creditable 2-2 draw, Vojak scoring both goals.

In the early stages of the campaign, Garbutt was battling to some extent against what he saw as his players' inferiority complexes, a feeling that they were not yet fit to compete on the same stage as the stars playing for the northern clubs. Napoli lay thirteenth out of eighteen teams in the league.

A short time into the New Year, Garbutt prepared them for the match against Genoa (or Genova 1893 now). Genova 1893 were strong, sat proudly at the top of the table and Garbutt knew only too well they would prove exacting opposition. Many of the players Garbutt had brought to the side had gone; only Moruzzi, Barbieri and Levratto remained. De Prà, 'his' goalkeeper, was injured and would take no part. One face that had remained was instantly recognisable to Garbutt, that of Renzo De Vecchi, the 'son of God' he had signed for Genoa so early after becoming Genoa's coach. The two men shared a genuine affection, had experienced so many highs and lows, glory and defeat. A firm handshake was followed by an embrace between two legends of the infant Italian game.

On this occasion, the pupil came out on top as Genova 1893 retained their place at the head of the *Serie A* table with a 2-1 win. Garbutt's professional pride was hurting at the defeat, but it could not have been lost on him that he had been instrumental in making De Vecchi the coach he had become.

All things considered, Garbutt's aim of moulding Napoli's talented individuals into a competitive unit was realised. In coming fifth, they had finished higher than well-established, illustrious teams such as AS Roma and Bologna, Pro Vercelli and Milan. They had won fourteen games, drawn nine and lost eleven. They had scored more goals than they had conceded (sixty-one as opposed to fifty-one) and had even convincingly beaten the eventual champions Ambrosiana 3-1. In scoring twenty goals for the season, Vojak provided the Neapolitans with a new hero.

Garbutt's employers were more than happy with the way things had gone in his first season and were now looking for him to build upon the foundations he had created. Napoli traditionally awarded medals to their squad at the end of the season. One player, Athos Zontini, was unable to attend the ceremony to collect his medal personally and so his father made the journey to collect on his behalf. Garbutt welcomed the senior Zontini warmly and the two men engaged in a lively conversation on all manner of subjects. Garbutt asked the man where he lived and listened intently when Signor Zontini told him of Bagnoli Irpino and of the town's beautiful natural environment, its pure mountain air and surrounding forests.

Anna Garbutt suffered greatly from asthma and her husband knew that clean, crisp mountain air was bound to be healthier than that of a city such as Naples. Garbutt enquired of Signor Zontini if it was possible to travel to Bagnoli Irpino and back in a single day. Upon being told that such a journey was indeed possible, Garbutt decided that he would take a look at the place for himself.

He was impressed with what he saw and, upon returning to Anna, eagerly painted an image of the municipality. She, in turn, was entranced by the description and the couple made the decision to take up residence. Soon after their arrival, Anna sat at home by an open window to take some fresh air and heard the laughter and singing of a young girl. Anna struck up a conversation with the eight-year-old Maria Concetta Ciletti, the daughter of a family living in the same apartment block, and over the course of the next days and weeks the two became firm friends, Maria only too eager to help the English lady with some small domestic tasks. For her part, Anna enjoyed the company that Maria provided while William was away from home attending to his duties with Napoli. William and Anna had no other children after their son Stuart, and Maria could be seen as the daughter Anna yearned for. The relationship was of mutual benefit. Maria's mother had died the year before and there is no doubt that Anna provided the love of a mother that she missed so badly.

Satisfied that his wife had found contentment in her new surroundings, Garbutt was able to focus all of his energies into Napoli's forthcoming season. This began with a narrow 1-0 home win in late September 1930, Pro Vercelli providing the opposition. A week later Garbutt made the familiar journey to Genova where he witnessed an emphatic 4-2 victory to the *rossoblu.* Another victory and defeat followed, after which Napoli hit a rich seam of form that saw them gradually climb the *Serie A* table. Garbutt led his team to nine wins, one draw and only one defeat following the win against Livorno in Naples on 26 October 1930. The 2-0 home victory against Casale on 11 January 1931 saw Napoli reach the dizzy heights of joint second in the table, along with AS Roma.

The home supporters were ecstatic, believing Garbutt, Sallustro, Vojak and company were going to bring them the *scudetto,* the shield given to the champions. Unfortunately for Garbutt and his team, results became more erratic, culminating in a disastrous final nine-game spell at the end of the season from which Napoli were able to glean maximum points on only two occasions. One of these defeats came following their home game to Ambrosiana on 24 May 1931. With ten minutes of the second half remaining, a number of home supporters invaded the pitch, kicking and punching both the referee and opposition players. In line with the league's rules, the game was awarded *a tavolino* to Ambrosiana, and Napoli were ordered to play their next home fixture at a neutral venue.

Despite the poor end to the season, it was another successful one for the consistent Vojak who contributed twenty goals. Napoli's eighteen wins, one draw and fifteen defeats would see them finish sixth. The northern monopoly on titles continued unabated, with Juventus of Turin being crowned champions of Italy for the third time (the first of an impressive five titles in succession).

As the 1931–32 season dawned, optimism among all those connected to AC Napoli was high. Fifth and sixth place finishes in the previous two seasons had built a firm foundation on which the club could build. Garbutt had worked with roughly the same squad of players for two seasons now and both he and the players understood what was required. In light of that, the campaign was an anti-climax. Despite a promising ten-game unbeaten spell in the middle of the season, stretching from the 20 December 1931 to 28 February 1932, Napoli ended a disappointing ninth.

There were high points, including Sallustro's two goals which earned Napoli a 2-0 home win on 7 February against the eventual champions, Juventus. But these were too few and far between, however, for the southerners to make any real impact. Strong home form (ten wins, six draws and only one defeat) had been mirrored by a frustrating away record (three wins, three draws and eleven defeats). Crowd hero Sallustro top-scored with twelve goals although Antonio Vojak had a poor season by own relatively high standards. He and Mihalic contributed nine goals apiece.

After the disappointment of 1931–32, Garbutt might have expected the directors to look for a new man to lead them into the new season. It was to their credit and ultimate reward that they retained faith in the Englishman and reaped the benefits in 1932–33.

Garbutt's fourth season with the Neapolitans began on 18 September 1932 with a home match against Lazio. With only three minutes of the game gone, the referee awarded the home team a penalty. Vojak confidently placed the ball on the spot and smashed the ball past the goalkeeper's despairing dive.

Three minutes had elapsed in the second half when Sallustro guided the ball effortlessly into the net to send the home crowd into a frenzy of delight. Two minutes later, the same player made sure that no comeback was possible by giving Napoli a 3-0 lead. Fantoni scored a consolation goal for Lazio but the points were safe.

Such was the style and assuredness of the manner of the victory that the home supporters once again allowed themselves to dream of a successful season.

Sallustro also scored in Napoli's next game, a 2-2 draw away to Triestina. Indeed, he scored seven goals in the first five games and it is little wonder that his adoring public demanded he represent the national side, seeing Pozzo's preference for the legendary Giuseppe Meazza of Ambrosiana as yet another example of northern prejudice against the *Mezzogiorno*. Garbutt's team remained unbeaten for the first nine matches, a run that included defeats of both Juventus and Milan. Victories against the northern sides always tasted sweeter!

Going into the game against Bologna on 4 December 1932, Napoli headed the table, having played nine games, winning six and drawing three. They had scored twenty-two goals and conceded only nine. But as had been the case in previous seasons, Bologna was to prove Garbutt's nemesis. The unbeaten run ended in a 3-1 defeat which saw his side surrender their position at the summit of *Serie A* to Juventus, a lead they were unable to regain. The final game of the season on 25 June saw Napoli travel to Milan to play Ambrosiana who were second. A thrilling battle ensued, Napoli taking the lead, Ambrosiana equalising, Napoli racing away to a 4-1 lead before the home side pegged them back to make the score 3-4 with ten minutes remaining.

Milan had a large Neapolitan population and it must have seemed as if the bulk of them were in the stadium for the game given the roar when Napoli secured the victory with a fifth goal four minutes from the end. Defeat for Bologna on the same day meant they and Napoli ended the season on forty-two points.

Napoli would not better the third place finish they earned that day for many years to come. Antonio Vojak was back to his goal-scoring best with a haul of twenty-two goals, ably assisted by Sallustro's best-ever return of nineteen.

The next season, 1933–34, would be Garbutt's penultimate at the helm of the Neapolitan side. It began on 10 September 1933 with a poor performance and dreadful result, a 4-1 defeat at Triestina. Another defeat, this time to Ambrosiana in the third game of the campaign, left Napoli sitting miserably at the bottom of the league. This was both a new and humiliating experience for Garbutt and one which he was determined to overcome.

One of the few bright spots in an otherwise dismal beginning to the season was Napoli's 2-0 home win against champions Juventus on the opening day of November 1933. A penalty from Vojak and a further strike by Buscaglia ensured Napoli's run against Turin's finest would continue.

Christmas Eve would see a dramatic about face in fortunes for Garbutt's squad. As the Napoli faithful made their way to the ground to watch their team take on Milan, they could have been forgiven for doing so without great optimism. Napoli went into the game lying a disappointing ninth. However, from then until the end of the season they played twenty matches, winning fifteen, drawing three and losing only two, away to Juventus and Alessandria.

In the final round of *Serie A* matches before Italy hosted the 1934 World Cup, Milan met Napoli on 29 April. With only five minutes remaining and Napoli leading 1-0, crowd disturbances again ensured the game could not come to its natural conclusion. Again the authorities were called upon and the points awarded to Napoli in an *a tavolino* win. For the second successive season, Garbutt had led his side into third place, this time in their own right, and their total of forty-six points gave them a four-point gap to fourth-placed Bologna.

This can only be seen as a tremendous achievement for Napoli. Only the northern footballing giants of Juventus as champions (for the fourth time in succession) and Ambrosiana could better them. Vojak's haul of twenty-one goals equalled that of Meazza although goals from other players were relatively few. Rossetti contributed seven and Sallustro five.

The only cloud on Garbutt's horizon was the disappointment of witnessing his beloved Genoa relegated for the first time to *Serie B*. His old club endured a dismal season, gaining just twenty-four points from their thirty-four games, and duly finished second from bottom. One can only imagine what a huge blow this demotion must have represented to the supporters of Italy's oldest club.

The 1933–34 season had finished early to allow Vittorio Pozzo time to prepare his national squad for the second World Cup, scheduled to take place on

Italian soil between 27 May and 10 June. The holders, Uruguay, refused to defend the trophy in retaliation at the failure of the European nations to attend the inaugural Jules Rimet tournament held in Uruguay four years earlier.

William Garbutt would have loved to have seen England participate in the Jules Rimet but the Football Association had withdrawn from FIFA in 1928 and were ineligible to enter.

Napoli's Stadio Giorgio Ascarelli was chosen as one of the eight venues to host matches. Goalkeeper Giuseppe Cavanna was the only Napoli player to make Pozzo's squad. Such was their dominance of domestic football at this time that Juventus provided no fewer than nine of the twenty-two-man squad. This time Pozzo did not call upon Garbutt for assistance in preparing the *Azzurri* for the challenge ahead. Needless to say the Italian coach had gained vast experience in the twenty or so years since he had first asked for Garbutt's help, but it was also politically unthinkable that a foreigner, particularly an Englishman, be invited to the showpiece about to take place on Italian soil.

The *Azzurri* opened the tournament with a thumping 7-1 win over the United States in Rome. The Stadio Giovanni Berta in Florence on 1 June was the venue for the next match, with opponents Spain giving the Italians a much tougher examination. Extra time failed to provide a winner so both teams were required to play again in the same stadium the very next day. In searing heat, Meazza gave Italy an early lead which they managed to cling to.

Just two days later, Italy faced the Austrian 'Wunderteam' in the semi-final in Milan's Stadio San Siro. Sixty-thousand spectators witnessed a goal by the *oriundo* (an immigrant of native ancetry) Enrico Guaita settle the tie in the Italians' favour. Guaita would soon be the focus of a great controversy when he fled across the border into France rather than wear the uniform of the Italian armed forces after being called up to serve in the war in Ethiopia. Some commentators noted with disdain that certain *oriundi* were selective as to when they did and did not wish to be considered Italian.

Czechoslovakia stood between Italy and glory in the final game played in Rome on 10 June. This was the Italian team's fifth match in only fifteen days. When the Czechs took the lead after seventy-six minutes it appeared as if the physical demands made upon the *Azzurri* had proved too much. Just as Italian hopes appeared to be evaporating, however, a goal by another Italo/Argentine, Raimundo Orsi, ensured the game went into a nail-biting extra thirty minutes. After only five minutes of extra time, Bologna's Angelo Schiavio scored what proved to be the decisive goal. Italy had won the World Cup, and in so doing had provided Mussolini and his followers with a priceless propaganda coup.

Garbutt's sixth and final season in charge of Napoli – 1934–35 – proved to be disappointing. Hopes had been high that consecutive third place finishes would provide a foundation on which to build. However, a lack of goalscoring prowess (Vojak scoring ten out Napoli's thirty-nine league goals) hampered the southerners. Their season petered out into mid-table mediocrity. Juventus again won the *scudetto*, an amazing fifth year in succession.

The Englishman's farewell to Naples was undertaken in much the same manner he had left Genoa: without recriminations, amicable on both sides. He had served the Neapolitans well, built a team capable of holding their own against the northern clubs and while not yet ready to break the monopoly these teams had on the championship title, had got Napoli closer to it than any of those who had gone before him. No Napoli coach would be able to match Garbutt's achievement of a third place finish until the Argentine Bruno Pesaola in 1965–66. As with his departure from Genova, Garbutt left Naples with the genuine affection of the people of the area. While not legally in a position to adopt Maria Concetta Ciletti, William and Anna had all but made Maria one of their own family and rescued her from abject poverty. Such a gesture was not lost on the people of Naples, for whom family comes above all else.

Chapter 8

Athletic Bilbao and a New Challenge

Garbutt's next footballing challenge came from a wholly unexpected source. His achievements in Italy might have been ignored by the English press but with Napoli's domestic success earning them a place in European competitions, Garbutt's achievements as a coach were well known to those connected with football throughout the continent.

One such was the President of Athletic Bilbao, José Maria Olabarrìa. The club, based in Spain's Basque region, had strong links with England, Bilbao Foot-Ball Club having been formed in the final years of the nineteenth century by British miners and shipyard workers.

The popularity of football was assured by the sons of the Basque middle classes returning from their studies in England. Garbutt was to follow a path well trodden by Englishmen before him. Messrs Shepherd, Barnes, Burton, Pentland and Kirby had all preceded him as coach of Athletic, with varying degrees of success. Without doubt the most successful was Frederick Pentland.

Born within months of each other in 1883, Pentland and Garbutt's lives followed a similar path in many respects. Both had played for Blackburn Rovers before heading for the continent to seek a career in football seeing as none was available at home. Whereas Garbutt chose Italy (or Italy chose him), Pentland had the misfortune to make his way to Germany where he intended to coach the Olympic team. In the wrong place at the wrong time, Pentland was interned at the outbreak of the Great War.

In some respects, Pentland's success reflected that of Garbutt's with Genoa. In 1923 Bilbao won the Spanish Cup, the Copa del Rey, under his guidance. Following this, he coached other Spanish clubs before returning to Bilbao in 1929 and leading them to La Liga, the Spanish championship, and Copa del Rey double triumphs in 1930 and 1931. The Copa del Rey was won four times in succession from 1930 to 1933.

Garbutt may have viewed the success enjoyed by Pentland as something of a double-edged sword. Pentland's success may even have influenced the Bilbao directors to offer the post to another successful English coach in the first place. Ever the realist, Garbutt was well aware that Pentland would be a hard act to follow and if he were to deliver anything less than the Spanish title it would be seen by Bilbao supporters (fed on a diet of success) as a failure.

The move to Spain posed a great personal challenge to Garbutt. He was moving not only to a country about which he knew little if anything, but essentially to a nation within a nation. After more than two decades coaching in Italy, Garbutt may well have been able to understand and make himself understood in certain areas of Spain but the Basque region was certainly not one of these. The language there was an impenetrable, unfathomable mystery to Garbutt.

Luckily for him, and as was the case when he first arrived in Italy some twenty-three years earlier, a number of team members spoke sufficiently good English to enable Garbutt to get his footballing message across.

Garbutt's move to Bilbao in late October 1935 coincided with fascist Italy's invasion of Ethiopia. Mussolini and his followers were only too aware that the regime required what the historian James Joll has termed a 'second wave of the Fascist revolution'[39] to rekindle public enthusiasm. The invasion conveniently distracted the Italian public's attention from the domestic economic difficulties which beset them. Despite Ethiopia's plea for protection from her fellow League of Nations members, Britain and France displayed little concern for the fate of the African nation. Realpolitik dictated that the need to court Mussolini as a potential ally in any future conflict with Germany would ensure that both would turn a blind eye to the invasion. Shortly after moving to Bilbao, Garbutt received a letter from Vittorio Pozzo. Dated 18 November 1935, and typewritten in English on FIGC notepaper, the great man wrote:

I saw you training and coaching in Genoa, Rome and Naples, I had you as an assistant during the Olympic Games in 1924, where the Italian National Team shaped so well; and I remember you interrupting your career to serve your country during the Great War. You did very well indeed. I can testify for it. You have got a great knowledge of the game and you know how to deal with players and directors. I can sincerely say you are one of the most deserving sportsmen I have met in a career of thirty years. If my name can serve you as a reference, use it.

Vittorio Pozzo

In Bilbao, Garbutt inherited a talented squad, a number of whom had either played for the national side or would do so in the future. One of these, Angel Zubieta Redondo, made his professional debut as a fresh-faced seventeen-year-old during the 1935–36 season. His impressive performances under Garbutt's tutelage made him the youngest player ever to pull on the national jersey of Spain, just seventeen years and nine months, in a game against Czechoslovakia. As with many other young men playing in Spain at the time, Zubieta's career was cruelly cut short by the imminent civil war.

Garbutt's happy knack of coaching sides that enjoyed prolific marksmen continued at Bilbao. Guillermo Gorostiza had been top goal-scorer in the Spanish league in 1930 and 1932. Top scorer in 1931 was another Athletic striker, Agustin Sauto Arana (better known as Bata). Bata scored 108 times in 118 games for Bilbao yet made only one appearance for the national side. Both Gorostiza and Bata enjoyed great success with the Basque team, helping them win four championship titles and four *Copa del Rey.*

Garbutt's Bilbao experience began with an away tie to Oviedo on 10 November 1935 and resulted in a point for the Basques following a 3-3 draw. His early days coaching in Spain were certainly an eye-opener for him. So much was new; the attitude of the Spanish crowds, the refereeing standards, the media, directors and so on.

Garbutt knew he had to adapt quickly if he was to succeed and started as well as he could have hoped when the following week Bilbao met Betis at the San Mamès Stadium (known as *La Catèdral*) in front of their own passionate supporters. The result, a resounding 7-0 victory for Garbutt's men, would set the tone for the rest of the games at home that season, with Athletic proving to be invincible. In eleven games they amassed an impressive forty-five goals, conceding only fourteen.

The following week away to Hèrcules, a match they lost 1-0, indicates perfectly the dichotomy of the season. While no opposition could live with Athletic at San Mamès, the Basques were a mundane side on the road, winning three, drawing three and losing five of their eleven matches – hardly championship material.

Ten games into the campaign, Bilbao played host to Real Madrid on 12 January 1935. The two teams sat at the top of the table, Madrid on fourteen points, Athletic on thirteen. Already the match had taken on great importance, and while it may have been somewhat premature to see it as a title decider, defeat would have made winning the championship all the more difficult for the vanquished side.

Garbutt was determined that his Bilbao would not walk off the field defeated. His determination proved well founded for Athletic won the game with a solitary goal, scored by Gerardo after twenty minutes.

In the following weeks, Madrid and Bilbao swapped positions at the head of the table, first one then the other. Game seventeen of the twenty-two match season, played on 15 March, was to prove crucial. Madrid went into their game, away to Racing Santander, at the head of the table on twenty-three points. Athletic, in second place and with a deficit of a solitary point, would play at home to Hèrcules.

Garbutt's team duly gained two points by beating their opponents 5-3 while Real lost to Santander by the odd goal in seven. With five games remaining, Garbutt was aware just how crucial it would be for his team to remain focussed on the challenge ahead. His concerns were well founded for Athletic themselves would lose away to Santander on 29 March. Despite this setback Madrid were unable to capitalise as they were also losing, in their case to Oviedo.

Both sides had convincing wins the following week: Athletic defeated Barcelona 5-2 at San Mamès and Madrid won 4-1 away at Osasuna. In the penultimate game of the season, Athletic (on twenty-eight points) had to face Madrid (one point behind) in the Spanish capital in what could well have proved to be the title decider. The points differential was maintained, however, when Athletic twice battled back from a goal down to draw 2-2.

Even in the final game of the season it was not possible for Garbutt and his men to relax. Were they to lose at home to Osasuna, and Madrid won away to Betis, Real would be crowned champions. On 19 April 1936, Athletic Club went on to defeat Osasuna 2-0. Madrid's result was therefore rendered irrelevant, but as it happened they were held to a draw by Betis.

William Thomas Garbutt, three times coach of the champions of Italy, was now the coach of the champions of Spain. Remarkably, his exploits were still not considered to be newsworthy in his own country. This triumph could well have signalled the beginning of another successful era for both Garbutt and Bilbao. The Englishman had everything at his disposal to become as significant a figure in the Basque capital as Frederick Pentland – a wealth of coaching experience, financial backing, a young talented squad and passionate home support. It was not to be, however. History would deprive both coach and club of the opportunity, for the Spanish nation would soon be plunged into a disastrous, destructive civil war.

At the end of the season, and after the proud Basques had exhausted every possible opportunity to celebrate their team's championship, Athletic Club paid Garbutt's air fare to return to Italy to collect the family that had remained behind in Naples.

Maria, who lived with husband Bill in Nott-
inghamshire before passing away at the beginning
of August 2009, explained that William intended to
collect his wife Anna and her and return as a family
to Bilbao to resume his duties as coach.

Back in Naples, Garbutt kept abreast of the
deepening crisis in Spain in as much detail as the
biased fascist Italian newspapers would allow. In
many respects, the situation in Spain resembled that
of pre-fascist Italy in that politics were hopelessly
polarised. Following big swings to the left-wing
Popular Front coalition in the elections of 1936, the
left were afraid of a right-wing coup, while for their
part, the right wing were convinced that a social
revolution was imminent. A military uprising in July
1936, with General Franco at the helm, led rapidly
to civil war. Once again, Garbutt's life was turned
upside down by conflict. On this occasion, football
was arguably one of the least important victims of
the loss of normal daily life caused by war. Needless
to say, however, Garbutt did not return to Bilbao.
Instead, he remained in his beloved Italy where,
despite the state-sponsored xenophobia which the
fascist authorities wished to see permeate every
aspect of the country, Milan became the latest club to
seek an improvement in their fortunes by employing
the Englishman.

Chapter 9
Moving to Milan

Following his return to Genova in the autumn of 1936, Italian clubs were soon aware of his availability. Garbutt began negotiations with Juventus, but the AC Milan President, Emilio Colombo, made his move while others dithered and contacted Garbutt, the two men meeting to discuss the possibility of the *Mister* taking control of team affairs for the *rossoneri*.

Garbutt was finally beginning to enjoy the fruits that came with being a championship-winning coach in both the Italian and Spanish leagues. A club like Milan was prepared to pay handsomely for a man of his experience and the contract terms were generous by the standards of the day. One thing the club could not deliver, however, was the quality of air or climate which the Garbutts enjoyed in southern Italy. As an asthmatic, there was no possibility of Anna living there, and so she and Maria lived in Vara Inferiore, a picturesque mountain village some twenty-five kilometres from Genova.

Garbutt lived out of a suitcase in a hotel and the two would travel to see him whenever they could.

The thirteen-year-old Maria Ciletti was by now a permanent fixture in the Garbutt household, her father realising that the English couple could offer his daughter a much better quality of life than he could ever dream of. Besides, not for a moment did Signor Ciletti think that state of affairs was permanent. Little could he have known, in 1936, that in a few short years, Europe first, then most of the world would once again be embroiled in the horrors of total war.

President Colombo displayed his ruthless streak in sacking the incumbent Milan coach Adolfo Baloncieri just ten games into the 1936–37 season. The four campaigns prior to this one had seen Milan finish eleventh in 1932–33, ninth in 1933–34, joint tenth in 1934–35 and eighth in 1935–36. This was an unacceptable series of results for a club of Milan's stature. The ten games under Baloncieri's charge in this latest season had seen no real improvement, and with a third of the season completed, Milan languished a dismal tenth out of sixteen, on only ten points.

In one of those ironies that seem to permeate football, Garbutt's first game in charge of Milan would be an away game against, as the fascists insisted on calling the club, Genova. Eleven games into the season, on 6 December 1936, William Garbutt once more made his way to the Marassi stadium he knew so well; to the venue in which he had created champions and moulded the careers of now legendary internationals. The game was settled in Milan's favour by a first-half goal from Cossio. The following twenty matches with Garbutt in control yielded an impressive twenty-six points, a tally which saw them rise at one stage from tenth to second in the *classifica*, just two points adrift of Bologna.

Despite the best efforts of Garbutt and his side, however, Milan were unable to maintain the surge and their final game of the season, away to Bologna on 16 May 1937, was little more than a coronation of the new champions of Italy. There seemed to be a symmetry at work when Garbutt realised that his last games in charge of Milan would also be contested against Genova, played at the end of the league season in the semi-final of that season's *Coppa Italia*. On the final Sunday of May 1937, the two sides met in Milan. Genova were stunned when Boffi gave Garbutt's side the lead after only two minutes but went on to equalise through Figliola in the second half. Extra time failed to separate them and they met again on 1 June in Genova.

On this occasion it would be Genova who struck the first blow with a goal from Marchionneschi after sixteen minutes. Boffi restored parity after half an hour and the scores remained at one apiece at the end of ninety minutes. With only two of the one hundred and twenty minutes of the game remaining, Marchionneschi broke Milan hearts by scoring a second.

With no time to respond, Milan had lost. Garbutt's supreme professionalism and his innate competitive spirit saw to it that he could take no consolation from witnessing his beloved Genova defeat his current charges. Despite this, he was happy to see the *rossoblu* lift the *Coppa Italia* when they defeated Roma 1-0 in the final played in Florence on 6 June. Garbutt had book-ended his career as coach of Milan with games against his true love, and despite the semi-final defeat, it had been a good season for both him and Milan. Garbutt had risen to the challenge set him by the Milan directors at the start of the campaign and restored some pride and stability to the team, guiding them to a creditable fourth. The decline of the *rossoneri* halted, Garbutt's thoughts had already turned towards his next move.

Genova 1893's demise following their relegation at the end of the 1933–34 season had been short-lived. Too strong for *Serie B*, they romped home as champions and set about restoring themselves once again as a force to be reckoned with among Italy's elite clubs. Genova 1893's president by now was Juan Claudio Culiolo, a man of considerable ambition and the wealth to realise these ambitions.

Following Garbutt's relative success with Milan, President Culiolo contacted Genoa's former coach and discussed the possibility of his returning to the club for the 1937 season. In all likelihood, Culiolo did not need to be much of a salesman to persuade Garbutt to take on the role. Genova 1893 was, after all, Garbutt's club. It was, and would always be, his first love in football.

The history of the man and of the team were intertwined. A return to Genova also suited the *Mister* for domestic reasons; living Milan's Maltecca hotel on *Corso Buenos Aires*, despite its luxury, was not to Garbutt's taste. Going back to the city where his name was revered would enable him to live with Anna and Maria in Vara Inferiore, a place he called home and had first visited as far back as 1927.

News of the *Mister's* return soon spread around the bars and cafès of Genova and was greeted enthusiastically by the *tifosi* of Genova 1893. Finally, here was the man they were convinced would deliver the much-awaited tenth *scudetto*. In the decade since Garbutt's departure to AS Roma in 1927, Genova 1893's fruitless quest to return to their glory years had seen them employ no fewer than eight coaches. The club yearned for stability.

But the 1937–38 season became a case of 'so near, yet so far' for Garbutt and Genova 1893. Despite a seven-game winning run in January and February 1938 which enabled them to claw their way to within a point of the eventual champions, Ambrosiana, they were eventually forced to settle for a joint third-place finish along with Milan.

Genova's poor home form had been their ultimate undoing. Of the fifteen matches played at home, the *rossoblu* had been able to muster only seven victories, a poor return when compared with the thirteen home wins enjoyed by Ambrosiana, ten by Juventus and nine by Milan.

What made this state of affairs all the more frustrating was the fact that Genova's away form was in direct contrast to the results suffered at Stadio Luigi Ferraris (the Marassi having been renamed in honour of the great Genoa player who had fallen in the Great War). On their travels, Genova triumphed on an impressive eight occasions, compared with only three wins for Ambrosiana and four each for Juventus and Milan. Genova's attackers were in potent form also; in scoring fifty goals for the season, they were second only to Ambrosia on fifty-seven.

Chapter 10

The World Cup and war clouds

The third World Cup, held in France from 4–19 June 1938, was a competition that reflected accurately the divided world that existed at that time. Both Argentina and Uruguay refused to enter, in protest at FIFA's decision to award the finals to France. The South Americans had assumed that, as Italy had acted as host in 1934, the venue would automatically switch to their continent. For the Europeans, Spain would not enter due to the civil war and the Anschluss (the annexation of Austria into greater Germany by the Nazis in March 1938) put paid to Austrian hopes. The British football associations, still on the outside looking in, were ineligible, feeling perhaps that their obvious superiority made the tournament somewhat superfluous. Two of Garbutt's Genova team, Mario Genta and Mario Perazzolo, made the Italian squad but would frustratingly fail to be involved in any of Italy's matches.

Matches involving Pozzo's *Azzurri* became the focal point for demonstrations by exiled Italian and anti-fascists. The hostility seemed to galvanise the Italians, however, and Pozzo skilfully fostered a siege mentality among his squad. Following a narrow 2-1 win over Norway in Marseille, the Italians were drawn to face France in Paris on 12 June. As both France and Italy wore blue shirts, lots needed to be drawn to decide which team would play in their first-team kit. Under normal circumstances a white kit would have been second choice; clearly these were not normal times. Having drawn the short straw, the Italians strode out in front of the 58,000 crowd, the vast majority of them French, in the black shirts made infamous by the fascists back home. As if this was not a sufficiently provocative gesture, the Italian squad gave raised arm fascist salutes during the pre-match anthems.

Proving too strong for their opponents, Pozzo's men marched into the semi-final where they were drawn against the flamboyant Brazilians. At this stage of the tournament, the Italians enjoyed something of a stroke of good fortune. The Brazilian coach, Pimenta, made the strange decision to leave the prolific striker (and tournament top-scorer) Leônidas out of the starting line-up, declaring, 'I am resting him for the final.'

Such optimism proved premature as a 2-1 victory for the Italians ensured that they would defend their trophy against Hungary in the final to be played at the Stade Olympique de Colombes in Paris on 19 June. The Italian nation rejoiced as the *Azzurri* triumphed 4-2 in the final. Needless to say the fascist leadership celebrated with them.

With the onset of the Second World War, the World Cup would not be contested again until Brazil was chosen to host it five years after the conflict had ended. The Italians thus held on to the trophy from 1934 until 1950. Dr Ottorino Barassi, an Italian official (who had helped organise the 1934 tournament in Italy and would help construct the 1950 tournament), hid the Jules Rimet trophy in a shoebox under his bed for fear that it would fall into the hands of German occupying forces in Rome.

It seemed that no sooner had the triumphant *Azzurri* returned from France with the Jules Rimet trophy safely in their possession than the insatiable thirst of the Italian public for their football demanded to be satisfied once more. Only one week after the final, on 26 June 1938, Genova met Sparta Prague at the Luigi Ferraris in an early forerunner of European competitions. Garbutt's men won the day 4-2 and in Prague the following week Genova gained a 1-1 draw thanks to Agostini, the *rossoblu* goalkeeper, making a fine save. Genova progressed to the next round where they defeated the Romanians, Rapid Bucharest, 3-0. Despite losing 2-1 in the return leg, Genova progressed to the semi-finals. In front of thirty thousand passionate Genoese on 24 July, Genova beat Prague's other team, Slavia Prague, 4-2. The European adventure ended in difficult circumstances the following week when Genova lost 4-0 in Prague.

The defeat was costly for Garbutt for other reasons; after twenty-seven minutes Sergio Bertoni was seriously injured. Reduced to ten men (and further still to nine when both sides had a player sent off later) Genova ran out of steam.

The domestic season began on 18 September 1938, Genova losing 3-2 at home to Bologna. At the conclusion of the contest, Garbutt and Arpad Weisz, the Bologna coach, walked towards one another and, arms outstretched, shook hands firmly. Obviously unaware at the time, it was to be the last occasion Garbutt would ever set eyes upon his opponent. The two men had pitted their wits against each other on many previous occasions, winning some, losing others, but both enjoyed the contests and retained a strong respect for each other's abilities.

Like Garbutt, Weisz was a champion coach, having led Ambrosiana-Inter to the inaugural *Serie A* title in 1930 and more recently, back-to-back championships with Bologna in 1936 and 1937. A Hungarian Jew, Weisz fell victim to fascist Italy's race laws introduced in July 1938. Together with his family, wife Ilona and two children Roberto and Clara, Weisz was forced to leave home. They made their way first to Paris then to Holland.

When the Nazis occupied Holland, the four made a final journey to Auschwitz. Ilona and the two children died in October 1942, Roberto aged twelve and Clara only eight. Arpad Weisz, champion coach in Italy, died in Auschwitz, a broken man, on 31 January 1944.

Two names which appeared on the Genova team sheet in the opening-day fixture against Bologna did so for the very last time. Both Uruguayan *oriundi,* Emanuel Figliola and Carlos Servetti, no doubt concerned at the worsening political situation in Europe, followed the example set by fellow *oriundo* Guaita some years earlier and fled home to South America via France.

This cowardice, or commonsense, depending on one's point of view, gave currency to those who viewed *oriundi* as nothing more than the mercenaries of Italian football. Whatever, the hasty departures proved costly to Garbutt's side. Both were able footballers. Servetti, a forward, had scored nine goals in only thirteen games in the previous season. Figliola is, perhaps, remembered for other reasons.

On 29 May 1939, the American magazine *Time* reported:

> *Eager to bolster its team for the coming futeból (soccer) season, Rio de Janeiro's Vasco de Gama, one of coffee-growing Brazil's eight major-league futeból teams, tried last week to buy a famed Uruguayan player named Figliola. To their dismay, the Vasco de Gamas discovered that Figliola had already been signed up by a football club in Genoa, in coffee-hungry Italy. More eager than ever, they called Genoa [and] offered to buy his contract. Prompt was the reply; the Italian Football Federation would permit the Genoese club to release Figliola if the Brazilian club would pay for him with coffee beans.*[40]

As in previous seasons, Garbutt was once more frustrated by the Jekyll and Hyde characteristics displayed by his players. This was a team capable of scoring nine times against Ambrosiana and Torino (two sides that would go on to be runners-up and third in the championship respectively) in the space of nine days in April, then draw and lose the next two games to lowly Bari and Livorno. In the plus column, by scoring an impressive fifty-three times, Genova would be second only to Ambrosiana who reached fifty-five. Strong not only in attack, Garbutt coached the side with the meanest defence in the league, conceding a miserly thirty goals in thirty games.

Chapter 11
War and Internment

With the spectre of war looming once again over Europe, William and Anna made the decision to return to England in the final summer of peace. Although he usually made the journey back to his native Lancashire at each season's end, this time the trip was made for an altogether more urgent purpose.

The Garbutt's son, Stuart, had returned to England aged twenty-four in 1936 and had recently joined the army. Anna felt the deep anxiety common to all mothers whose sons are about to join one of the armed forces whenever war seemed imminent.

For his part, William questioned his son's sanity in volunteering, until the younger Garbutt reminded his father that he had acted in exactly the same way twenty-four years earlier. Indeed, on his return to England, William Garbutt had enquired of the war office if there was a means by which he might profitably serve his country if needed. On this occasion his country did not call; there was no demand for the services of a man in his mid-fifties.

Prior to his departure, aware that he was still under contract to Genova, Garbutt spoke to President Culiolo and asked for compassionate leave. That approval was given so readily may be due in some small part to the fact that he was able to convince Culiolo, and the other directors, that his assistant, Ottavio Barbieri, was ready to assume control of team affairs in his absence.

Garbutt had been quick to recognise the talents of Barbieri as a player, and now some twenty years later had supreme confidence in his coaching abilities. Approval granted, the Garbutt's booked their train passage and made their way to England. Soon after their arrival the international situation turned for the worse.

Time and again, Britain and France had sought to appease Hitler over his expansionist plans in Europe, concessions having been made on issues ranging from German rearmament and the annexation of Austria to the transfer of the Sudetenland from Czechoslovakia to Germany.

Hitler gambled that the British would not fulfil their pledge to support Poland in the event of a Nazi invasion. The signing of the Nazi–Soviet pact on 23 August signalled the removal of the final barrier and in the early hours of 1 September 1939, Germany duly invaded Poland. At 11.15 am, on 3 September, William, Anna and their relatives, along with millions of fellow Britons, sat grim faced and attentive around radio sets and heard Prime Minister Neville Chamberlain declare:

I am speaking to you from the Cabinet Room at 10 Downing Street. This morning the British Ambassador in Berlin handed the German Government a final note stating that unless we heard from them by 11.00 a.m. that they were prepared at once to withdraw their troops from Poland, a state of war would exist between us. I have to tell you that no such undertaking has been received, and that consequently this country is at war with Germany.

Though the Italian peninsula would in due course become one of the most devastated patches of earth of any involved in the conflict, for the time being at least, things went on much as they had done. The Italian public's unquenchable thirst for football meant that the championship would kick off, impending global conflict or not, on 17 September 1939. With Garbutt in England, his assistant Barbieri grasped his opportunity and began to experiment with Genova's playing style, and an attempt was made to adopt the patterns of play made famous by, among others, Herbert Chapman's legendary Arsenal side.

Compared with the latest formations and tactics deployed by the top English sides, Italian football's continued reliance on a 'W' formation (operating with two full backs, three midfielders, two wingers and three forwards) appeared 'antiquated'.[41] As might have been expected, 'Barbieri's Genova' took time to adapt to their new formation and tactics, which were something of a radical departure. An opening day 1-1 draw away to Fiorentina was followed up by a 3-0 home win against Bari, a 1-1 home draw against Milan, a heavy 4-1 defeat in Rome to Lazio, a 5-3 home win against Novara, with a defeat by the same scoreline in the next game against Bologna. A 3-2 home victory against a strong Juventus side at the end of October 1939 showed that Genova could compete with the best using their new system, but the players struggled to find any real consistency. Following a 6-2 hammering of Venezia on their own ground, Genova were in joint second place, along with Ambrosiana-Inter, Lazio and Venezia, one point behind leaders Bologna on eleven points.

Despite Italy and Germany having signed the 'Pact of Steel' in May 1939, Garbutt and his wife felt safe enough to return to Genova in time for the home game against Napoli on 19 November, with the team celebrating the *Mister*'s return with a 2-0 victory. They had always intended to return to Italy. This had been their home, by and large, since 1912 and they enjoyed a wide circle of friends. Stuart was now serving in the army; besides, they had someone else depending on them back in Italy – seventeen-year-old Maria, who had remained in Vara Inferiore when they had returned to England.

As the Italian domestic season unfolded, Pozzo, the national coach, had become convinced of the need for the *Azzurri* to adopt the new methods of play employed by Genova and a friendly international to be played against Germany in the Olympic Stadium in Berlin on 26 November 1939 was chosen as the match to introduce the change. The national side's line-up for that game reflected the fact that Genova were seen as the architects of the new method, for Pozzo chose seven Genova players in the starting formation: Marchi, Sardelli, Genta, Battistoni, Perazzolo, Neri and Scarabello.

The signatories to the 'Pact of Steel' kicked off in front of forty-five thousand supporters, with Neri giving the Italians the lead on fifteen minutes. Hitler's annexation of Austria had provided sporting, as well as economic and territorial, benefits to the Germans; Binder (an Austrian) equalised five minutes later. Again Italy gained the upper hand, through De Maria on twenty-seven minutes, only for Binder to restore parity shortly after. As the game wore on, the Italian team's lack of experience (only four players had made more than one international appearance prior to this game) and the fact that the method of play was so relatively new (even Genova had played only nine league games prior to the match against the Germans) meant the Italians were overrun and the hosts plundered a further three goals (including Binder's hat-trick) to win easily. Not surprising then that one prominent Italian football historian concluded that the experiment 'was a failure'.[42]

Genova's next three league games saw a return of only one point. Garbutt intervened and acted decisively, instructing Genova to return to a style of play with which the players were more comfortable. The experiments with 'the method' were abandoned for the time being at least. Results began immediately to improve. A 2-1 away win to Reggiana in the

Coppa Italia on Christmas Eve was followed by six wins and a draw in the next seven league games. A 4-0 crushing of Lazio on 11 February 1940 meant Garbutt had led Genova to the summit of the Italian championship, a position they shared with Bologna, both on twenty-six points.

Genova's next game, contested at Novara's Stadio Littorio seven days later, has gone down in the history of Italian football. Genova 'won' the game with a goal scored by Sergio Bertoni after thirty-three minutes. The score was hotly disputed by the Novara players, who were adamant that Bertoni had handled the ball.

However, it was a technical error by the referee, Scarpi, that would go on to cost Genova dearly. Bizarrely, Scarpi failed to notice that Bertoni had kicked off both halves for Genova. Novara won an appeal and the Italian Federation duly ordered a rematch to take place on 8 May. Genova won only two of their next six games and this lack of form and injuries to key players (Genova's Italian international Giovanni Battistoni broke his leg in a game against Milan on 4 February) began to take their toll on the squad and Genova lost the re-match 3-1.

Deflated, and with morale at a low ebb, Genova hobbled to the end of the season, gaining only three points from their final four matches. After a season that had held such high promise only a dozen or so games earlier, Garbutt could only watch frustrated as they finished a disappointing joint fifth with Torino, on thirty-three points. Ambrosiana-Inter clinched the title with forty-four points.

If the championship had proved ultimately disappointing, Genova's *Coppa Italia* exploits offered the club a glimmer of a trophy. The win against Reggiana in the first round had been followed up by victories away to Napoli (1-0 on 7 April) and Modena (2-1 on 28 April) and a 2-0 victory against Bari in a semi-final played at the Luigi Ferraris. This game, played on the 9 June, would be the last played on Italian soil in peacetime. The following day, after months of dithering and hesitation, Mussolini gambled on his own future and that of his country by joining forces with Germany.

Italy's declaration of war on Great Britain and France meant that Garbutt's career as coach of Genova was effectively over. He was the subject of much well-intentioned advice around this time. Genoa's President Culiolo, the British Consulate, friends in Italy and family back home in England, all urged William and Anna to flee the country at the first available opportunity.

Three crucial factors led the Garbutt's to ignore the advice and make the fateful decision to remain in Genova. Garbutt was not only the first, he was the most famous and successful professional coach in the history of Genoa Football Club. With the final of the *Coppa Italia* due to take place against Fiorentina in Florence in a matter of days, he was determined he would be the one to lead his team out.

Secondly, as guardians, both William and Anna felt a real sense of responsibility towards Maria. The seventeen-year-old, living in Vara Inferiore, was very much reliant upon the Garbutts and as an Italian citizen, it would have proved virtually impossible for the English couple to have taken her out of the country by legal means, and far too dangerous to attempt to remove her by any other.

Finally, Anna's own health was precarious and may not have been up to the stresses and strains of a hurried departure. In a scribbled note written on 6 June 1940, William managed to get news out to family back in England. On notepaper headed *Genova 1893 Associazione Calcio*, Garbutt wrote:

> *Dear Jim and Maggie,* (James and Margaret Speet, his brother-in-law and sister)
> *Nance* (William's pet name for his wife Anna)
> *cannot travel so we are staying on. Stuart got back from the scrum, received a wire yesterday.*
> *Things do not look too rosey* (sic), *but we have been through it before & never been licked.*
> *Love to all, Willie*
> *Perhaps after, someone from Genoa will call on you at least we hope so, with a note from me.*
> *Keep smiling*

And so, for better or worse, William and Anna remained in the country that had been their home for the best part of twenty-eight years. Unable to make the journey to Florence to lead his side in the *Coppa Italia* final, Garbutt was reduced to following the game in the same way that millions of Italians followed *calcio* each week; by listening to the commentary of the famous broadcaster, Niccolo Carosio, on the radio.

Rarely can Garbutt have endured the frustration he must have felt that day, unable to influence the game in any way. He had faith in Barbieri's ability, but this was his Genova team and he felt he knew how to get the best from them. Genova lost the final to a goal by Fiorentina's Celoria after twenty-six minutes. The ability to put things into perspective was one of the few benefits of getting older, however, and Garbutt soon realised that defeat in a football match paled into insignificance when compared with the present dire circumstances facing his family and the world at large.

Holed up in their residence in Vara Inferiore, William, Anna and Maria were at least able to provide each other with much-needed mutual support and the village provided a haven from the crazed environment of Genova. The Garbutts had made an annual pilgrimage to Vara Inferiore since 1927 and it had always been the Englishman's sanctuary from the stresses and strains of managing a professional Italian soccer club.

Equally important was the fact that the healthy mountain air did nothing to worsen Anna's asthma. Little wonder that William and his family wished to stay here for as long as the state of war between Italy and Great Britain lasted. The Italian authorities viewed the matter very differently. It may seem strange to suspect that a professional soccer coach in his late fifties could be involved in the murky world of espionage but paranoia was a trait shared by many nations during the war and the Italians were unwilling to take chances. Garbutt had military experience and the proximity of Vara Inferiore to Genova, a port of great strategic importance, was also a factor.

Garbutt was so well known in Vara that his presence no longer warranted attention; the Italian authorities understandably wanted him somewhere he would be kept under constant scrutiny by the prying eyes of inquisitive locals. Towards the end of June 1940, instructions were issued to the prefecture in Genova that Garbutt should be apprehended and be interned. As June stretched into July, telegrams passed between the Ministry of the Interior in Roma and Garbutt's employer, Genova 1893. President Culiolo, in particular, was acting as a mediator in the process, keen to protect the interests and safety of the ageing Englishman but eager also not to antagonise the authorities.

Events currently taking place in Britain did nothing to improve the lot of British citizens in Italy. Following Italy's declaration of war, Winston Churchill, upon assuming the mantle of Prime Minister from Joseph Chamberlain on 10 May, had ordered that all Italians living in Britain be interned, demanding the police 'collar the lot!'[43] a knee-jerk reaction that conveniently ignored the fact that many of those to be locked up had lived in Britain for many years and may even have fled persecution from Mussolini's fascists.

Before long, Garbutt was forced to accept the inevitable and he realised the need to give himself up to the police in Genova. With Culiolo once again acting as a go-between, William Garbutt, accompanied by his anxious wife Anna, made the journey from Vara Inferiore to face an uncertain future in Genova, and who knew where beyond? As the instantly recognisable Englishman walked into the police headquarters, those he passed turned their heads in a double-take, in an effort to convince to themselves that it was indeed the icon of Genovese football they had seen.

Those officials whose duty it was to deal with him treated him with the utmost respect. There were no harsh words as was often the case with other detainees, no intimidation, either physical or verbal. Treated respectfully or not, it still came as a real shock to Garbutt when he was arrested as an enemy of the Italian people, and the utter helplessness and awful reality of the situation facing him began to hit home.

Fascist bureaucracy satisfied, Garbutt was led away to Genova's Marassi prison. From a window in his cell he was able to gaze longingly upon the nearby stadium (just five hundred metres away) at which he had created championship-winning teams, coached players who would go into folklore and where he himself had become a legend of the Italian game.

As the war progressed and Italian sovereignty gave way to the far more brutal Nazi regime, the Marassi prison would become an infamous focal point of a number of terrible atrocities. In May 1944, Obersturmbannführer Friedrich Engel, as head of the Genova branch of the SS, ordered that fifty-nine Italians (mostly young men) be taken from the

Marassi and executed in retaliation for a bomb blast at a cinema that killed five German marines. In his defence, the 'Butcher of Genoa' as he became known, claimed that Hitler himself had demanded he 'repay attacks resulting in death' and that for every German death, ten Italians should die.[44]

Mercifully for Garbutt, while his stay in the Marassi would prove uncomfortable, it would not end in such random slaughter. But William was not able to have his wife by his side to help him through his ordeal. As an Irish national (and therefore not in conflict with the Italians) Anna was told she was free to walk away from the police headquarters any time she chose. Turning her back on her husband was not an option Anna Garbutt would have considered for an instant.

As soon as she had got over the initial shock of seeing William being led away, she began to deal with the practicalities facing them. If it was not possible for Garbutt to be freed to be with her, she would do whatever it took to be with him, even if this happened to be a concentration camp. With access to lawyers provided by Genova Football Club, Anna Garbutt wasted no time in drafting an appeal to be forwarded to the authorities.

The fact that the appeal was a legal document does not lessen its emotive power. Anna stressed that the couple had lived in Italy for the previous twenty-eight years with the exception of the time spent in Britain during the Great War and Garbutt's season-long sojourn in Spain. She reminded the authorities that the couple had had ample opportunities to leave Italy, and had ignored advice from the British Consulate to follow such a path, due to Garbutt's 'great sympathy for the Fascist regime'.

Anna encapsulated Garbutt's service to Italian football in the petition; mention is made of his leadership of Genova, whom he led to South America on a phenomenally successful tour, AS Roma, Napoli and Milan, and of his work with Pozzo on behalf of the Italian national team, contributing in some way to the remarkable success enjoyed by the *Azzurri* in the global game. If Garbutt's magnificent achievements in, and on behalf of, the Italian game were not enough to impress the authorities, Anna took the opportunity to stress the couple's advancing years and provided medical certificates signed by doctors giving evidence of her poor health.

Almost two weeks dragged by with Garbutt penned in the Marassi prison, during which time his health began to deteriorate worryingly. There can be no doubt that he was treated with respect by all those around him; still, the absence of his wife and daughter was beginning to take its toll. Conditions inside the prison were basic, bordering on primitive, and the general lack of hygiene was something that even President Culiolo's financial offerings could do little to improve, or to protect his well-known employee from.

Anna enquired daily about her husband's well-being, and a lack of information added to the stress and anxiety of the situation for all concerned. At least Garbutt's ill-health appears to have jolted the authorities out of their inertia. Whether they were afraid of having the demise of one of the country's most famous football managers on their hands can only be guessed at, but in very little time a decision was reached as to Garbutt's next destination. The authorities had also relented, allowing William and Anna to be reunited, a decision which brought the couple great relief.

The decision to allow the couple to remain together was something of a surprise as the general trend at the time appeared to separate husbands and wives, sending them to different areas, particularly in the case of Jewish families.[45]

Whereas Garbutt himself had always been the author of his own destiny, choosing which of the continent's top football sides he would manage, his future was now in the hands of the fascist authorities. On this occasion, Garbutt's next port of call was not to be a cosmopolitan city such as Milan or Rome, or a bustling port along the lines of Genoa or Bilbao, but an isolated backwater called Acerno, some fifty-five miles from Naples and in close proximity to the Eboli made famous by Italian writer and anti-fascist Carlo Levi's novel, *Christ Stopped at Eboli*.

In 2009, a journey from Genoa to Acerno would be tiring for a healthy individual. In 1940, at the height of summer, in ill-health, and made in the company of guards, the same journey can only have been torturous for the Englishman and his loyal wife. When they eventually arrived after what must have seemed like an eternity, William and Anna felt as if they had stepped back in time. In Acerno there were no grand houses or theatres (a favourite pastime for

Anna) and what passed as restaurants were strictly functional, not designed for pleasure like those they had regularly frequented in the great cities of Europe.

Their immediate accommodation needs were met in the town's lodgings (it would be inaccurate to call it a hotel). No mind, Garbutt and his wife were so exhausted that they slept soundly for the short time they were there. It might have lacked in grandeur, but Acerno was a typically attractive mountain village.

Importantly, the locals were friendly towards their new guests and when more permanent accommodation was found for the famous football coach and his wife, they received gifts of furniture, basic foodstuffs and other items to make their stay more comfortable. Officially, internees were forbidden from fraternizing with the local population, but this was yet another regulation by and large ignored.

Ironically, Acerno was the perfect environment for Anna. At more than seven hundred metres above sea level, it enjoyed fresh mountain air and the entire area seemed to be surrounded by the chestnut trees which played such an important role in the local economy. In time, Acerno would find itself at the epicentre of the bloody battle between the Allied and retreating German forces but for the time being at least all remained peaceful and calm and Garbutt was able to rest and restore his health.

In quieter moments, he expressed gratitude for the way events had panned out. He shuddered to think of what might have been: transportation to a concentration camp without his wife, or even worse. He understood that whatever privations he and his wife suffered they were no more than those affecting the average *Acernesi*, and life took on a regular, if somewhat mundane, pattern. Each day William and Anna were expected to report to the local police station, where the Carabinieri would officially complete whatever paperwork was necessary to satisfy fascist officialdom.

Like all other internees, the Garbutts were free to move around the village until about 6 p.m. but were strictly forbidden to leave the boundaries of Acerno without having first sought official permission. This particular curtailment of their freedom weighed heavily on William and Anna at first but as the war wore on, they adapted, and through necessity, conditioned themselves to their confinement.

One aspect of their lives remained a constant source of anxiety for the Garbutts – the precarious state of their finances. While William Garbutt undoubtedly earned a comfortable living from the game, then, as now, it was the star players who were able to command stellar salaries. A popular saying in Italy goes something along the lines, 'he found bread, but he did not find America' and this could be said to be true for Garbutt's earnings from the game.

What money the Garbutts had saved while living in Genova was beyond their reach, having been sequestrated by the authorities. In yet another gesture of compassion and goodwill towards an employee they held in such high esteem, Genoa Football Club continued to pay Garbutt's salary for a period following his arrest and internment.

In common with other internees the Garbutts received a small stipend from the authorities while living in Acerno. This amounted to the princely sum of eight lire per day for William as the head of the household and a further four lire for Anna as his wife (to give some indication as to the value of this allowance, one kilogram of pasta would have cost in the region of two lire). The Garbutts received a further fifty lire per week which enabled them to pay their rent.

Despite the obvious financial hardship they faced, William and Anna had appealed for Maria to be allowed to rejoin them in Acerno.

As if having an extra mouth to feed on such a meagre income would not be difficult enough, Maria, as an Italian citizen, was not entitled to receive the three lire per day stipend paid to children of 'regular' internees.

Nevertheless, the trio were a family and would stand together to face whatever hardships and deprivations the war could throw at them. As they had done some three months earlier by allowing Anna to share her husband's internment with him, the authorities listened sympathetically to the mutual plea made by both 'parents and child' and Maria rejoined William and Anna in Acerno in November 1940.

This proved especially beneficial in that Maria, having been born in the nearby village of Bagnoli Irpino, took on the role of translator to the English couple and provided a pathway through the thick local dialect.

At least in the early days of their confinement the trio had no great difficulty finding food. Living in a rural area helped as local farmers always had surplus produce for sale. As the war wore on, the black market was often able to supply what could not be procured by more legitimate means. William's main gripe was the shortage of pipe tobacco. The omnipresent pipe, which had become Garbutt's trademark, continued to perch between his teeth, but much to his chagrin, fulfilled its true purpose with less frequency.

So, while William and Anna missed the variety that Genova, Rome and Naples could offer, there was an obvious trade-off in that life in Acerno was far more healthy and relaxing. If one had to spend the war interned, there were certainly worse places to be than Acerno in the summer of 1940.

But there was one particular aspect of life under internment with which William and Anna found increasingly difficult to cope – the enforced isolation from family and friends. Communication with the world they had known before their confinement was now limited to the occasional heavily censored letter from England made possible by the good offices of the International Red Cross. In a letter sent home dated 30 December 1940, the Garbutts wrote:

Dear Maggie & Jim, We are interned at above address (Presso Municipio, Acerno, Prov. Salerno, Italy) since August. We are quite well & are waiting for news from you.
Regards to all, Willie and Nance

The few letters they received from home displayed a similar brevity and lack of any real information. One example is a pre-printed letter headed 'War Organisation of the British Red Cross and Order of St. John (Prisoners of War, Wounded and Missing Department), which was sent by William Garbutt's brother-in-law through the Red Cross in Geneva. Under a section headed 'The Enquirer desires news of the Addressee and asks that the following message should be transmitted to him,' is typewritten:

Dear Willie,
Pleased to hear from you. Maggie, myself, Jack &
all well.
Regards, Maggie & Jim

On the horizon was the new Italian football season. This would be the first time since 1915 (when Garbutt's career had been disrupted by the Great War) that he would not be involved in preparing a team for a new campaign. He felt the disappointment keenly, and though he kept abreast of the comings and goings of the teams in the league, he knew that things could never be the same again. He missed the day-to-day involvement with players, ensuring they would begin the season in the best possible physical shape, working on tactics and discussing potential new signings with the president. These were now nothing more than distant memories of a life he had once lived.

Temperatures began to fall and summer gave way to autumn. The restrictions on movement meant

Garbutt had little to do other than take leisurely walks around Acerno and its immediate environs and to read the newspapers in the local bar. Given the political climate, it was no great surprise when the headlines screamed out that Italian troops had invaded Greece. Newspapers and radio, the mouthpieces of fascism, triumphantly announced that with Il Duce in control a rapid victory was assured.

By this stage, however, it was not only Garbutt and his fellow internees who preferred to gather the latest information from other sources, including the British Broadcasting Corporation; many Italians joined them. They were given a very different picture, one which must have been heartening for those keen to witness the demise of fascism.

The invasion of Greece took place on 28 October 1940, timed to celebrate the anniversary of the March on Rome. Suffering from a severe lack of preparation, the assault seems to have been doomed to failure from the outset. Every aspect mitigated against the Italian forces, from the weather – the imminent rainy season ensured below freezing temperatures (Italian troops once again being supplied with totally inadequate clothing and footwear) – to the severe limitations of the Albanian infrastructure, from where the invasion would commence.

The fact that fascist foreign and military policy was so incoherent and erratic was largely down to Mussolini who immersed himself in triviality and sought to control every minor detail of the campaign. Equally, his senior chiefs of staff displayed their weakness in being either unable or unwilling to question their leader's judgement.

Within a week of the ill-fated invasion, Greek troops were pushing their foe back into Albania and for the next three months the poorly equipped Italians found themselves fighting a rearguard action. By the spring of 1941 the situation was so bad for the Italians that their German allies were left with no alternative other than to move their own forces to provide support for Mussolini. Greece was invaded and her brave army capitulated within a fortnight.

The repercussions of this humiliating setback for the Italians were profound. If Hitler's confidence in Mussolini had not been exhausted before this debacle, it certainly was now. Similarly, senior Italian military staff began to harbour grave doubts concerning the increasingly irrational decision making of Il Duce. One can understand why historian Denis Mack Smith comments that 'the rickety structure of fascism was increasingly laid bare to the light of day.'[46]

If summer and autumn in Acerno had been agreeable to the Garbutts, winter proved a much more brutal affair. William, Anna and Maria struggled against the seemingly endless days of sub-zero temperatures. Whereas the climate had been beneficial to Anna's asthma during the warmer months, it was now proving to be a potent enemy. Her husband was sufficiently concerned to write to the authorities once again, this time requesting a transfer to a milder climate, one less detrimental to his wife's health. Once again the fascist authorities considered the Englishman's appeal. To the couple's relief, the request was approved and the trio was informed that they would be moving to a town near Chieti, in Italy's Abruzzo region.

As with Acerno (and countless villages and towns just like it) Orsogna was considered an ideal location in which to accommodate enemy aliens or those Italians who displayed what the authorities considered to be anti-fascist tendencies. It was relatively isolated and its native inhabitants appeared to hold no overt political opinions. The town was a melting-pot, the population of the native *Orsognesi* swelled by refugees of different nationalities and religions. Despite the influx of outsiders, the locals were inviting to all. Anti-semitism may have been an official fascist policy, but it appears not to have been shared by the indigenous residents of Orsogna, who were aware of, and accepted, their new Jewish neighbours.[47]

Arriving at the latest town they would call home in the early months of 1941, the Garbutts could not have failed to have been impressed by the stunning scenery in every direction. Sat on top of a hill, Orsogna enjoys a panorama of the majestic Maiella Mountain to the west, the Gran Sasso to the northwest and the Adriatic Sea to the east. As had been their experience in Acerno, the Garbutts were met with respect and sympathy by the local population. Before long, word had spread around the scarcely believing townsfolk that one of the latest batch of internees was none other than *Il Mister,* the great English footballer and coach.

Before long, Garbutt had been persuaded to become involved in the coaching of Orsogna's youth team, and the young players of the town needed little encouragement to show off their skills to the famous personality living among them. After all, here was a man who, until only recently, had been instrumental in coaching sporting heroes such as De Vecchi, Barbieri, Volk, Bernardini, Vojak and Sallustro.

For his part, Garbutt enjoyed passing on the fruits of thirty-five years of experience to these enthusiastic youngsters, providing him as it did with some diversion from the essential boredom that was often the bane of many an internee's life.

The months of 1941 came and went, only the weather distinguishing one day from another. The Garbutts received the occasional all-too-brief written message from family in England assuring them of their well-being. William's involvement in the Italian professional game was limited to following events in the daily newspapers though he still took an interest in Orsogna's youth team.

As 1941 was approaching its conclusion, events were about to take place that would turn the current European-based conflict into a global one. Just before dawn on 7 December 1941, Japanese aircraft attacked the American fleet at Pearl Harbour. Four days later, Churchill heaved a sigh of relief as Hitler declared war on the United States, thus bringing an end to American isolationism and ensuring her entry into the war.

Predictably, the cold weather of an Orsognese winter played havoc with Anna's health, not only in terms of her asthma, which she had endured for many years, but also with a variety of ailments. In letters she wrote to relatives, Anna complained gently of a 'groggy knee'.

The letters made no mention of the fact that she had suffered terribly from dental problems for a number of months and, in line with the requirements placed upon internees, needed to seek permission from the authorities to leave Orsogna to receive treatment from a dentist.

Early in 1942, the Garbutts received news which gave their spirits a much needed boost. Their son Stuart, writing from England, informed them that they had become grandparents. His wife Ivy had given birth to a baby boy, Barry William, on 1 February. The joy the couple felt on hearing the news was marred only by the fact that they were unable to see their first grandchild.

This domestic happiness surrounding William and Anna was to be short lived, however. In late March, Garbutt complained to his wife of constant headaches and told her that he thought he might be coming down with a bout of influenza.

After two days Garbutt lost completely the use of his legs and following a consultation with a specialist, Anna was given the shocking news that he had in fact suffered a stroke. There is little doubt that the stress and anxiety of the previous eighteen months had finally caught up with Garbutt. His incarceration, the uncertainty surrounding his family's future, the fact that his career and livelihood had been taken away from him and his understandable concerns for his wife's suffering, all played a part in the illness.

A letter Anna wrote to William's sister Maggie a month after the attack reveals the true seriousness of the situation. For two weeks after his stroke, Garbutt's health had been in a precarious condition. Despite the fact that Orsogna was relatively isolated and that the most able doctors would have been serving in the military, the Garbutts were somehow able to find a specialist to take charge of William's treatment. Anna was relieved to inform her sister-in-law that 'before long we had a decided improvement in his condition which up till (now) he maintains. He is now able to move his legs a little and we hope for the best. I think another month will see him on his feet again, fortunately he has good weather in his favour.'

Garbutt's illness placed a great strain on the uncomplaining Maria. Not yet twenty, the young woman now tended both her 'parents' through their health problems. Little wonder then that Anna's same letter home describes her as a 'godsend'.

Providing care to the sick coach was a difficult task. Having been fit and healthy his whole life, Garbutt did not take kindly to enforced rest and was impatient to get up and about. Despite his illness, old habits died hard. Anna's letter went on to thank Nellie (another of William's sisters) for the cigarettes she had sent him and which they were informed had lifted his spirits no end!

If life as an internee in an isolated town in the Abruzzi could be less than exciting, now that Garbutt was virtually bedridden his feelings of isolation and boredom were doubled. The days seemed to drag by even more slowly than they had before. As Anna had mentioned in her letter home, however, at least the weather was now in her husband's favour, and in time William was able to make tentative steps back to health.

By the time Garbutt wrote another letter home to his sister and brother-in-law in November, he was able to report an improvement in his health to the extent that he was doing a 'bit of wood chopping, so that's a good sign, makes me blow a bit.'

By the early months of 1943 it was obvious to many within Italy that the country could no longer fight. The Allies were putting together plans at the Casablanca Conference to invade Sicily later that year. Meanwhile, Galeazzo Ciano (Italy's foreign minister and Mussolini's son-in-law) was undertaking secret negotiations with the Allies in an effort to secure peace. Ciano's efforts were to no avail. For their part, the Allies were in no mood to discuss anything but total surrender and then with no one but Mussolini's successor.

As Allied bombing raids upon Italian cities became more and more common, Mussolini's attempts to stoke up an atmosphere of hatred against the British had the potential to put Garbutt and his fellow British internees living in Italy in real danger. These Britons were often sent to live in the very towns and cities subject to the heaviest bombing raids.

Mussolini's black propaganda extended to the newspapers and the daily *Popolo d'Italia* warned all Italians of the dire circumstances should their country be defeated by Britain. No scare tactic, no claim was too extravagant for the ailing *Duce*. Despite Mussolini's desperate attempts to rescue his doomed regime, and combined with the fact that the people of Orsogna held the Englishman in such high regard, Garbutt came to no harm during his time in the town. Shortly before dawn on 10 July 1943, the Allies invaded Sicily and, deluded as he was, even Mussolini must have realised his days were numbered.

In common with most of the other refugees in Orsogna, Garbutt regularly tuned in to BBC Foreign Service radio broadcasts to be kept informed of the latest developments in the conflict between the Allied and Axis powers. Though the penalties for listening to such broadcasts were harsh, most ignored the warnings. When circumstances allowed, Garbutt and his fellow internees would meet and discuss the latest news concerning the war and any progress being made by the Allies.

Recent months had given them great encouragement and cause for optimism. In October 1942, General Montgomery had routed Rommel at El Alamein and by May of 1943 German and Italian troops had been driven out of North Africa. Despite fundamental differences of opinion between the United States and Britain, the confidence and momentum engendered by these victories enabled Churchill to persuade President Roosevelt to attack the Axis powers at what was felt to be its weakest point, its 'underbelly', that is, Sicily. From 10 July to 17 August 1943, some half a million Allied forces personnel fought for control of the largest island in the Mediterranean in 'Operation Husky'. By the time one hundred thousand Axis troops escaped to mainland Italy across the Straits of Messina on 17 August, the political situation in Italy had changed beyond recognition. Mussolini had constantly sought to reassure his subjects that Rome would never be bombed.

When this very thing happened for the first time on 19 July, the political repercussions were tremendous. Senior fascists finally accepted that Mussolini's dictatorship was to all intents and purposes at an end. The fascist Grand Council met on 24 July and duly voted to ask the King to restore those powers to parliament which had been gradually eroded by Mussolini since his accession to power in 1922.

The following day, King Vittorio Emanuele advised the once omnipotent Mussolini that Marshal Pietro Badoglio would henceforth take over as Prime Minister with immediate effect. Incredibly, the creator of Italian fascism was promptly arrested. The transition was carried out with such remarkable ease that one can only wonder how the whole apparatus of the fascist state had survived for so long. According to Mack Smith:

By midnight, the news had spread through Rome and the whole complex fabric of fascism, which people had taken to be so strong and durable, disintegrated in minutes. Even the leader's own newspaper, the Popolo d'Italia, far from calling on Italians to oppose his relegation, meekly accepted the change of regime as entirely logical and, on its front page, simply took out Mussolini's name and replaced the usual photograph of him with that of Badoglio.[48]

On 3 September, the British 8th Army landed at Reggio Calabria on the 'toe' of the Italian mainland to continue the pursuit of its foe. On the same day, Marshal Pietro Badoglio signed an armistice with the Allies. The signing was not announced to the public until five days later, at 6 p.m. on the 8 September, first by Allied Commander in Chief, General Dwight D. Eisenhower, followed by Badoglio himself to the Italian public an hour later. Eisenhower announced:

The Italian Government has surrendered its armed forces unconditionally. As Allied Commander in Chief, I have granted a military armistice, the terms of which have been approved by the governments of the United Kingdom, the United States and the Union of Soviet Socialist Republics.

Chapter 12
Confusion and Tragedy

The vast majority of the war-weary Italians were jubilant at the news, believing that this signalled the end, or at least the beginning of the end, of their nation's involvement in the conflict. Sadly, this was not to be and the Italian peninsula would continue to be ravaged and to be the scene of many terrible wartime atrocities for many more months to come. The news of the armistice came as no surprise to Hitler who had long held doubts about the appetite of his Axis partner to see the battle through to its conclusion. In fact, the Germans had been preparing for just such an eventuality and as soon as the armistice was declared, steps were taken to occupy the eighty per cent of Italian territory not under Allied occupation.

Events were taking place at such a breathtaking pace that confusion was bound to reign and for this, Badoglio has borne the lion's share of the blame. In his haste to flee Rome (along with the Italian royal family and heads of the army and navy Marshal Badoglio left the capital in a fleet of cars in the early hours bound for Bari in Allied-occupied southern

Italy) he failed both to give any clear direction to the Italian forces under his command and to ensure that the deposed Mussolini was handed over to the Allies.

Italian troops were informed only that they were no longer at war with the Allies, but nothing about how they should deal with Germans on whose side they had been fighting just the day before. Needless to say, the ruthlessly efficient German war machine grasped the initiative and within one week of the Italians laying down their arms, all manner of military equipment was seized by the Nazis.

It was not only guns and tanks that were of use to the Germans; more than half a million[49] former Italian soldiers were rounded up and transported to Germany to work in armaments factories, no doubt manufacturing weapons that would =be used on fellow Italians at some later date. British prisoners of war were also left dazed by news of the armistice. It is estimated that there were upwards of eighty thousand British and other Allied troops in Italy around this time.

Initially, the order was given for these men to 'stand fast' by senior officers who were under the misapprehension that their liberation was expected at any time. Some took it upon themselves to disobey the order and took flight from the camps (which had in many instances been abandoned by their Italian guards) in an attempt to escape either north to neutral Switzerland or south towards the advancing Allied forces. Others roamed the Italian countryside, hiding from the Germans and occasionally joining up with the Italian partisans groups that were now springing up. There are countless instances of Allied soldiers receiving food and shelter from Italian farmers and peasants despite the regular German declarations about what would happen to those found aiding fugitives. The Italian historian, Giuliano Procacci, accurately summed up the situation thus:

> *During these days of disbandment and chaos the Italian people's profound modest virtues of kindness and tolerance shone brightly. No soldier was refused civilian clothes, no Allied prisoner who found himself unexpectedly at liberty was refused shelter and help, no Jew was without a hiding-place. In misfortune the Italian people began to rediscover their old civilized qualities.*[50]

Perhaps it was the fact that these brave Italians were aware that the soldiers they were assisting had been taken prisoner while trying to liberate them, or maybe they saw it as the only realistic action they could take to show resistance to German or Italian fascism. Their actions are all the more inspiring when it is considered that the Germans were offering a financial inducement of £20 for each Allied serviceman given up, a fantastic sum at a stage of the war when many families were literally starving.

Badoglio's failure to ensure the former *Duce* was handed over to the Allies meant that on 12 September crack German paratroopers were able to stage a daring rescue of Mussolini from the mountain-top hotel in Gran Sasso, in the Abruzzo region, where he was being held. From there, he was spirited away to meet Hitler in Bavaria. By the end of the month he had once more proclaimed himself to be the leader of the Italian people, this time as head of the Republica Sociale Italiana, also known as the Salò Republic after the small town on the banks of Lake Garda in German-occupied northern Italy where the puppet government was based.

Garbutt listened to news of the British 8th Army's advance along the Adriatic coast with a mixture of excitement and trepidation. By early October, Montgomery's troops had reached the port of Termoli, just sixty-one kilometres south of Orsogna. By the end of the same month, the German military ordered that public notices should appear on the walls of the town warning locals that they should prepare to evacuate their homes. This was necessary because of Orsogna's proximity to the so-called Gustav Line, the defensive position that stretched across the whole of the peninsula, and behind which the German army waited for the inevitable onslaught being prepared by the Allies.

Knowing that German soldiers were present in Orsogna in such large numbers, Garbutt made the decision to destroy his British passport. He was only too aware that anyone in possession of such a document would have been in mortal danger. At best, Garbutt would have been transported to Germany, more likely he would have been shot without much discussion. According to Maria, Garbutt's main concern was to ensure that neither she nor Anna came to any harm. And so, without fuss or ceremony,

William placed his well-used British passport into the fireplace and put a match to it.

The Garbutts and Maria joined the human procession that was leaving Orsogna by any means available, whether by truck, train or on foot, carrying whatever possessions they could manage. In their instance, the trio attached themselves to a group of thirty or so people, travelling together to provide a semblance of security which in reality probably did not exist, and made their way north, away from the Allies and into German-occupied Italy. After stopping briefly at small towns and villages along the way, the group made the town of Imola (some twenty miles south-east of Bologna) in Emilia-Romagna their latest home.

The winter of 1943–44 was exceedingly harsh, the freezing conditions made worse by drastic food shortages which were affecting the general population. Food rationing, perhaps to be expected during any war, was exacerbated by the German occupation and the fact that food destined for the Italian people was plundered and found its way into the stomachs of German soldiers or even civilians back in Germany.

In Acerno or Orsogna the Garbutts had been able to supplement their meagre rations with the produce of local farmers. In Imola this was not the case. Similarly, Allied strategic bombing of the road and rail network in German-occupied Italy meant that it had become increasingly difficult to distribute what little food did exist. It was a thoroughly miserable time. The atrocious weather had also forced the postponement of the Allied advance. Even in good weather, the Italian terrain was easier to defend than attack, as the Allies were finding to their cost. Still bogged down on the Gustav Line, the German army was defending the narrowest part of the Italian peninsula. Much of the country to the north of the Allies was mountainous and the Germans again had an advantage over their enemy in that they held the higher ground.

A seemingly never-ending series of rivers was another natural obstacle the advancing Allies needed to overcome, a task made all the more difficult due to heavy rain. Finally, the lack of modern roads at the time meant that supply convoys were restricted to which roads they could use, running the risk of being an easy target for German troops.

The German retreat, under the command of Feld-marschall Albert Kesselring, was highly organised. Any infrastructure that may have been useful to the Allies was systematically destroyed in the Germans' wake. No road, railway line or bridge was left intact. Booby traps and minefields were laid to slow down the advance and cause as much devastation as possible, and forced Italian labour was used to create and reinforce the defensive positions which the Allies encountered at each stage of their advance. At an hour before midnight on 11 May 1944, the Allies were about to launch another massive offensive upon the Gustav Line and Cassino, a town crucial strategically to both the Allies and the Germans. Just two days later, the horrors of total war were about to enter the Garbutts' lives.

Staple foodstuffs such as butter, oil, milk and salt were all in desperately short supply. Between them, the Allies had virtually destroyed northern Italy's transport and distribution network and the Germans had stolen any serviceable vehicle for their own needs. It was against this backdrop of near starvation that Anna and Maria went out in search of food on a Saturday afternoon. Extreme hunger can make people do desperate things and take incredible risks, and that is what happened on 13 May 1944.

Romantic versions of the events of that day have it that Anna had gone to church. However, she was accompanied by Maria and it was a mortal need for food rather than spiritual nourishment that the two women were desperate to satisfy. Maria told how a woman working in a local factory had arranged to meet to give her food. As Maria and Anna made their way to where they had arranged to meet the woman they heard the familiar drone of Allied planes overhead.

It seems that there was nothing particularly unusual in this, the Allies having enjoyed virtually total command of the skies over Italy for some time. Maria relived the fateful day and told how she and Anna took shelter under a railway bridge to wait for the planes to pass overhead so they could continue. Both were looking forward eagerly to the meal they had been promised.

The next thing Maria recalled was a deafening explosion, literally, and a blinding flash. When she came to, all around her was a scene of total carnage, demolished buildings, fire, panic and mayhem. She looked around and saw Anna lying still, blood seeping from her mouth. As she gazed at the motionless body next to her she believed instinctively that the woman she had thought of as her mother for almost fifteen years was dead.

Though she was unaware of the significance at the time, the loud ringing in her ears was an indication that Maria's hearing had been severely damaged by the impact of the bomb, damage that would not be repaired until she was able to undergo an operation some years later. Dazed and confused, Maria hailed a young man passing by on his bicycle and got him to give her a ride back to the house she shared with William and Anna.

Garbutt had been aware of the raid and when he saw Maria's dishevelled state, and the fact that she was without Anna, his heart sank. Still in shock, and suffering severe pain in her ears, Maria's words tumbled out in a confused torrent, telling him of the promised meal and of the bridge and the explosion. Somewhere amid all the details were the words he had been dreading, that Anna had been killed.

Unable to accept what Maria was saying to be true, Garbutt insisted she show him where the two of them had been. When they arrived at the ruins that remained, all around them was in a state of frenzy. Survivors, clothes torn from their bodies, continued to walk around in shock and disbelief, while relatives and friends in tears were running around shouting names and asking others if they knew of their loved ones' whereabouts. Maria showed Garbutt as accurately as she could where she and Anna had been standing but the Englishman's wife was nowhere to be seen.

Garbutt took this as a sign that Maria must have been wrong; Anna had been merely stunned by the explosion, had regained consciousness while Maria was away, and must now be wandering close by in a confused state. Allowing his spirits to rise, Garbutt grabbed Maria by the arm and they made their way, along with a crowd of others, to the nearest hospital. When they arrived, the scene before them resembled a battlefield. Garbutt failed to receive the news that his heart yearned for. His wife was not on the hospital ward.

The two of them now made another journey, this time to the hospital mortuary. Maria told how they both walked tentatively along the long row of bomb victims, a mortuary attendant slowly lifting the blanket covering each of the bodies, with Garbutt hoping against hope that his wife was not among them. Finally, a blanket was lifted and Garbutt stared for what seemed to Maria like an eternity at Anna, his wife and companion of thirty-three years, before breaking down.

In all, fifty-two innocent civilians had died that early summer's day in May 1944. The bombing raid had been carried out by the 461st Bombardment Group, a part of the United States Army Fifteenth Air Force. A total of $92^{1}/_{2}$ tons, consisting of five hundred pound general purpose bombs, fell on this clear day, a mere twenty per cent of them falling within one thousand yards of their 'aiming point'.[51]

To add insult to the tragedy, it appears that the freight yards of Faenza, some ten miles south-east of Imola, had been the true target that day and that the huge tonnage of bombs dropped indiscriminately upon the terrified citizens of Imola had been destined for another town. The aircrew entry for this mission reads as follows:

5/13/44 Fifteenth AF
HBs continue interdiction in spt of ground forces.
670 plus B-17's and B-24's, mostly with fighter
escort, attack M/Ys at Trento, Bronzola, Fidenza,
Piacenza, Faenza, Imola, Cesena, Modena,
Parma, San Rufillo, Borgo San Lorenzo, Castel
Maggiore and Bologna, and hit railroad bridges at
Bolzano and Aviso. Ftrs sweep Bologna-Modena
area.[52]
(Abbreviations: HB – heavy bombers; Ftr –
fighter; M/Ys – Marshalling (freight) Yards)

When the Garbutts left Orsogna for Imola they had been supplied with false identity papers. William had taken the name Michele Attardo while Anna carried the papers of one Giovanna Cota, wife of Attardo. To have carried papers giving their true identities was out of the question while failing to carry any identification at all would have been to invite suspicion.

And so, though it broke William and Maria's hearts, Anna was laid to rest under the woman's name she had been using at the time of her death. It had not been possible to reveal the deception as

Imola was still under the control of the occupying German army and local fascist Italians. It was not until the mid-1950s that William and Maria were in a position to have Anna buried under her true name.

It was a desperate time for Garbutt. The war had taken the only career he had ever really known and now it had taken the love of his life. If it had been difficult remaining interested in life before the tragedy, now he fell into a complete state of despondency. There was precious little to eat, but he had no appetite anyway. Luckily for him, the ever-faithful Maria was on hand with her gifts of great compassion and care, and she coaxed him back gradually from the dark tunnel of despair into which he had fallen.

Days after Anna's death, after five months of intense fighting, the Allies finally broke through the Gustav Line. The town of Cassino was liberated but an appalling price had been paid. Nothing but ruins remained, a pattern that was to be repeated time and again as the Allies pushed the Germans towards northern Italy. The bodies of dead soldiers, civilians and animals lay where they had fallen and the air was thick with the stench of death and decay.

By 4 June, General Mark Clark's 5th Army was liberating Rome, the first European capital to fall to the Allies. Florence would be the next target, the Allies all the while pushing the German enemy northwards. The fall of Rome was a great morale boost both for the Allies and for the burgeoning Italian partisan movement.

The *partigiani* became increasingly emboldened and, often with the clandestine assistance of local peasants and Allied arms' drops, the partisans carried out such an effective military campaign that, in their desperation to rid themselves of the problem once and for all, the Germans adopted a programme of *'rastrellamento',* that is taking steps to clear a given area of forces deemed to be hostile by any means necessary. There are many recorded instances of innocent men, women and children being slaughtered by German troops as a reaction to the partisans' activities.

The Gothic Line was Feldmarschall Kesselring's last throw of the dice. A ten-mile deep fortification consisting of concrete reinforced gun pits, barbed wire, anti-tank guns and trenches, it was a formidable defence and this was even before Italy's natural barrier, the three-thousand feet plus peaks of the Apennines, was taken into account. Kesselring also ordered that his troops impede the Allies advance by destroying 'every bridge, every road, every tunnel, every power station, every port – all had to be blown to smithereens.'[53]

Despite the delaying tactics employed by the Germans, the Allies made steady progress and it seemed that it was only a matter of time before the Germans were expelled from Italy and William, Maria and millions of others would at long last be able to celebrate the end of the terror. A number of factors combined to ensure that the war would enter its sixth year, however.

From the very outset, the brilliance of Kesselring's

leadership and the tenacity and bravery of the German troops need to be recognised. In addition, there existed a long-standing difference of opinion between the Americans and British regarding the future direction of the war. For their part, the Americans (who had real concerns about Britain's long-term ambitions in the Mediterranean) wished to concentrate the Allied efforts in attacking the Germans through France and not Italy. Despite Prime Minister Churchill's best efforts, the United States held sway and large numbers of Allied troops were removed from service in Italy to take part in the invasion of Normandy in northern France as part of Operation Overlord.

Larger numbers of troops were also withdrawn from the Italian theatre of operations to take part in the invasion of southern France (including French troops trained in fighting in mountainous terrain) and to quell the state of civil war existing in Greece between communists and royalists. The depleted Allied troops in Italy carried this burden and, perhaps predictably, exhaustion became a factor. Finally, but perhaps most crucial of all, the Italian weather was about to change for the worse and the autumn rains would soon arrive.

These turned rivers into raging torrents and made roads impassable. Even the Bailey bridges which had played an essential part in the Allied advance up the Italian peninsula began to be washed away in the rains. As one British soldier serving in Italy at the time wrote home to his wife in early October 1944:

There's no sign of autumn yet. It is summer one week and, click, you're pitchforked into mid-winter weather. And I never slipped and sploshed in such mud in all my life. All the time the Italians are wandering back to shattered homes, looking over the wrecks of their houses. Many go barefoot.[54]

Field Marshal Alexander, the Allied Supreme Commander Mediterranean, decided that, given the conditions, it made no sense to continue on the offensive, but better to wait until the weather improved and mount an all-out offensive in the spring of 1945. No doubt this was a sound military decision, but it must have been incredibly frustrating for those civilians, such as Garbutt, living near the front line and so desperate for one last push to expel the Germans from the country. At one stage, General Clark's 5th Army had been a tantalising twelve miles from Imola before the onset of the rains had stopped them in their tracks. It was an agonising case of 'so near, yet so far'.

Christmas 1944 was not a joyous occasion for William Garbutt no matter how hard Maria tried to make it so. It was their first since Anna's death and her absence was keenly felt. The desperate shortages of food continued and the fact that the demise of the German army had been so close to being achieved two months previously made their presence in Imola during the festive season all the more painful. Letters from home were now non-existent and Garbutt often talked to Maria of his concerns for his family back in England. No doubt they too longed for some information.

Garbutt also felt tremendous guilt over the fact that he had not been able to inform his and Anna's son Stuart (or any of Anna's other relatives) about her death and he worried endlessly about how they would react when they eventually received the terrible news. In due course he would be able to impart this to his son in the most remarkable of circumstances.

Ever since the Allies had been forced to call a halt to the offensive the previous autumn, they had begun making preparations for when conditions would allow for a recommencement of hostilities. Troops worn down by relentless fighting were rested. Stocks of ammunition were built up to enable a full-scale onslaught to take place in spring when it was hoped that the weather would be much improved.

Anna's shocking death almost twelve months earlier had left Garbutt mentally scarred. Despite this, he knew that Maria had suffered more than he on that fateful day, at least in a physical sense, and so he did his best to comfort and reassure the young woman when he saw her distress as they both listened to the unmistakable sound of aircraft above them in the skies of Emilia-Romagna. Air-raid sirens had a similar effect upon both of them.

Monday, 9 April 1945 dawned bright with cloudless, blue skies. There had been a real improvement in the weather of late and the freezing temperatures and snow of the winter were becoming yet one more unpleasant memory. Shortly after noon, Garbutt again became aware of the drone of Allied aircraft overhead and his anxiety increased proportionally.

The noise he heard was aircraft belonging to the Mediterranean Allied Strategic Air Force preparing the way for the spring offensive that began in earnest on that day. Eight hundred and twenty five heavy bombers, followed by wave after wave of medium and fighter bombers, filled the blue skies and pounded the hapless German troops in their positions along the Lugo-Imola front line for an hour and a half.

Understandably, the Germans were staggered by the sheer weight of the relentless assault and almost immediately fell back to new defensive positions, carrying thousands of their injured comrades with them. Ever since July 1943 when the Allies had landed in Sicily, the German army had been fighting a rearguard action in Italy, and at each stage of the campaign had retreated only because of the tremendous artillery and aerial bombardment unleashed by the Allies.

After two years of this assault, morale was low even among the Wehrmacht. It was as if the entire German army had suddenly realised that they could not win the war. Faced by a seemingly endless barrage of bombs and artillery from the Allies and harassed by Italian partisans behind the lines, the Germans stared defeat in the face.

Chapter 13

Liberation and Genoa again

Just under a week later, on 14 April 1945, the honour of liberating Imola fell to Allied troops of the Polish 2 Corps. At long last, after almost five years of war, the day that William, Maria and countless other citizens of Imola had long waited for had finally arrived. As the Polish troops made their way into Imola, there were few people on the streets of the town to greet them. The locals recalled how fifty-two of their fellow citizens had perished under the Allied bombardment in the previous year and chose the relative security of their homes. Before long, however, excited shouts could be heard and it was obvious that these were the result of celebrations rather than anything sinister.

William and Maria soon joined the growing mass of people on the streets and allowed themselves the luxury of believing that peace had finally arrived. The pages of history might well have told a different story, however. In February 1945, Churchill, Stalin and Roosevelt had met in the Crimea at the Yalta Conference to review the progress of the war and to discuss how a post-war world might look.

Stalin named his price for joining in the war against Japan: that Poland should be included in the Soviet sphere of influence at the end of the conflict. It was a price that Roosevelt in particular was content to pay. Polish troops, from their leader General Anders to the lowest ranked soldier, were convinced that they had been betrayed by their British and American partners.

In the cruellest of ironies, Polish troops had helped to liberate Italians, incurring a huge number of casualties along the way, and yet they had in turn been consigned to their own subjugation. Neither Britain nor the United States could really have had any argument had the Poles chosen to lay down their arms and walk away from the battle. To their eternal credit, they continued the fight.

Within a week, Bologna joined the growing list of Italian towns and cities to be liberated. The once omnipotent Benito Mussolini was apprehended by partisans while trying to escape into Switzerland. He, along with his mistress Claretta Petacci, and Alessandro Pavolini, the fanatical secretary of the Fascist Party, were summarily executed and, on 28 April, dumped unceremoniously at the site of a disused garage in the Piazzale Loreto in Milan.

An angry crowd soon swarmed around the corpses and began to rid themselves of years of hatred towards the fascist regime, abusing the bodies and hanging them upside down as if they were grotesque statues.

The partisans had not chosen Piazzale Loreto as the location to leave the dead body of the former

Duce and his cohorts at random. Back on 10 August 1943, fifteen men had been shot dead by the Germans and Italian fascists, and their bodies left in a pile as if they had been so much refuse. The fascists guarding the bodies refused their grief-stricken families access to their remains. Following this moment the partisans vowed that the men would be avenged and that when the time came, Mussolini and fourteen others would hang in the very same spot whether they were dead or alive. Just two days later, perhaps not wishing to risk a similar fate to that suffered by his friend and fellow dictator, Adolf Hitler committed suicide.

On 2 May, the German army surrendered uncon-ditionally in Italy and six days later, when all of Germany's forces followed suit, Europe and the United States erupted in joyous celebration.

Though they continued to endure their own deep grief, William Garbutt and Maria had survived the war. They had survived, not only the dangers posed by Italy's German occupiers but also her own fa-natical fascists. They had survived the massive aerial bombardments inflicted by the Allies, not only on the German Wehrmacht, but also on innocent civil-ians. Though by no means unscathed, they had sur-mounted the deprivations that were an unavoidable aspect of war, disease, malnourishment, and in the case of Italian winters, intense cold.

Shortly after the Poles had liberated Imola, British troops entered the town. Garbutt was exhilarated to see the familiar uniforms of the British army once again. At the first available opportunity, Garbutt introduced himself to a senior British official. The official in question was initially surprised to hear what he took to be local speaking English, and in a Lancastrian accent at that.

Garbutt gave a potted history, how he arrived in Italy some thirty-three years previously to coach Genoa, and of his internment since the outbreak of hostilities in 1940. Ever the patriot, Garbutt offered his services to the British army in whatever capacity they felt able to use him. Somehow, news filtered back to England of the former professional footballer who had been interned in Italy for the entirety of the Second World War.

No doubt many readers who followed Blackburn Rovers and Woolwich Arsenal read the article in the newspaper and recalled the days in which the flying winger had played for their team. Another person reading the newspaper that day was Garbutt's daughter-in-law, Ivy. She immediately contacted the War Office and asked for their assistance in notifying her husband Stuart who was at the time still in the forces.

In a remarkable coincidence, Stuart was serving in the British 8th Army in Italy. The War Office played their part, and got word to him that his father was living in Imola. The younger Garbutt sought a travel pass to go and meet his father in the northern Italian town. And when Garbutt senior and junior met, with Maria alongside them, Stuart queried his mother's absence. The awkward silence told him all he needed to know. It was a highly emotional occasion for all concerned.

After another family reunion, this time in Maria's birthplace of Bagnoli Irpino, Garbutt decided that the time was right to make the journey back to England to see his family for the first time since before the outbreak of war. After obtaining a temporary passport, he spent time with Anna's family before making the trek north to stay with the families of his brothers and sisters.

It was never his intention, however, that the return was to be long term. Having spent all but four of the last thirty-three years in Italy (and none of those in England) Garbutt, despite the horrors of the war, still considered Italy to be his home. He also recognised that he needed a long spell of rest and recuperation and decided upon an extended break with his family in Lancashire.

With Garbutt firmly ensconced in England, Genoa contested the first post-war championship in the northern Italy league. It turned out to be a thoroughly depressing season as they finished a poor third from bottom after collecting a meagre nineteen points. Torino were crowned champions with forty-two points.

Towards the end of the 1945–46 campaign, senior figures within Genoa Cricket & Football Club (the Anglicised pre-fascist version had been proudly restored) began making preparations for the coming season. When the discussion turned to who would be the man to coach the team, one name came to the forefront, that of the *Mister*. Who else but the iconic figure of Garbutt could lead Genoa in the search for their tenth title?

Club officials duly made contact with Garbutt and discussed his thoughts on leading Genoa for the fourth time. There can be no doubt that Garbutt, now sixty-three, was intrigued by the challenge of returning to coach the team he loved above all others. After taking a little time to ponder the offer, *il Mister* had come to a decision – he would leave England and return to Italy.

Genoa's first opponents of the 1946–47 season would be Brescia, in a game to be played at the Stadio Luigi Ferraris on 22 September. The massed Genoa *tifosi* stood as one to applaud the now ageing English gentleman. Garbutt had dreamt of this day during the long period of his internment.

On this occasion, Genoa won at a canter by four goals to nil. Two of those goals were scored by Juan Carlos Verdeal, an Argentinean making his debut for the club. He was the product of a Spanish father and Italian mother, and Garbutt and the Genoa supporters alike were entranced by his dribbling abilities, skills which had persuaded Genoa to meet the six hundred thousand lire transfer fee demanded by his club Dos Caminos Caracas of Venezuela.

This season also saw the union of two of Genoa's other teams, Andrea Doria and Sampierdarenese, a fusion which resulted in Unione Calcio Sampdoria.

There was to be no fairy-tale end to the season for Garbutt or Genoa. Rather, it turned out to be another of unfulfilled promise from which the club gained just thirty-six points from thirty-eight matches, a haul which resulted in a position of joint tenth along

with Internazionale, Lazio and their new city rivals Sampdoria.

The misery for the Genoa *tifosi* was compounded by two derby-day defeats to Sampdoria, a humiliating 3-0 home defeat in November followed by a 3-2 reversal in March 1947. In reality, every team in *Serie A* that season was overshadowed by a growing force that swept virtually all before them. The Grande Torino side was utterly dominant, their tally of sixty-three points giving them a full ten-point gap over runners-up and city rivals, Juventus.

Torino's star forward, Valentino Mazzola, played in all thirty-eight games that season and ended up as *Serie A* top-scorer with twenty-nine goals (equalling the combined total scored by Genoa's top two scorers, Dalla Torre on sixteen and Verdeal on thirteen). In all, Torino scored an amazing 104 goals in the league that season, conceding only thirty-five.

By the end of the season, Garbutt was exhausted. In years gone by, his mind would already be thinking about the season ahead and plotting a strategy to meet the challenges it would present. He would have had in mind players he wanted the Genoa board to bring to the club and new formations, set pieces and tactics to work on.

This time, however, he found it impossible to think or plan ahead as he had once done, and could only contemplate a complete rest.

All too soon, however, the Genoa directors began to discuss the strategy for the coming 1947–48 campaign with him. In darker moments Garbutt was beginning to doubt his ability to compete with the top coaches of the day. Always a fighter, Garbutt was never one to back away from a fair battle, but he was honest enough to acknowledge that modern football was probably a game for men younger than himself. Somewhat against his better judgement it seems, Garbutt accepted the offer to stay on in the role of the Genoa *Mister* for a further season.

When the new season finally got underway on 14 September 1948, Garbutt felt somewhat refreshed. His spirits were given a lift when Genoa scored three goals without reply in their away game against Lucchese. The following Sunday yielded another two points for *rossoblu* when one of his former teams, Napoli, were beaten 3-2 in Genova.

After these two games, however, Genoa's famed inconsistency returned and the next five matches returned three defeats and two victories. When Genoa met Sampdoria on 16 November in the first of that season's derby games, Sampdoria took the lead after only nine minutes courtesy of an own goal by Cappellini.

The Genoa supporters present must surely have feared the worst and another derby-day defeat against their bitter rivals following the two inflicted upon them the previous season would have been more than most of them could have coped with. Their fears were without foundation however when the heroic Juan Carlos Verdeal leveled the scores on the hour. With only five minutes remaining, Trevisani scored the decisive goal to ensure that the bragging rights of the city belonged to the supporters of Genoa for the time being at least.

Consistency was a quality that Genoa still found elusive, however. The next two matches resulted in defeats, away to Internazionale then Pro Patria. A handsome 4-0 home win against Vicenza and a goalless home draw against Livorno completed Genoa's fixtures leading up to the Christmas break. Three days after Christmas, Genoa were awarded a 2-0 *a tavolino* victory at Bari, after the home supporters invaded the pitch to signal their displeasure at a goal they considered to be offside. Following this result, Genoa lay in a creditable sixth position in the league, only five points behind the joint leaders Milan and Torino, both on twenty points, and with half the season remaining for Genoa to mount a serious challenge for the title.

A disastrous succession of results helped Garbutt to come to a profound decision. From New Year's Day 1949 to 8 February, Genoa took just one point from seven games. They were beaten by Salernitana, Roma, Torino, Triestina, Fiorentina and Bologna. The only respite was a draw at home to Atalanta in the third game of the sequence.

The supporters were understandably in shock and, as supporters will, looked around the wreckage of the season for a scapegoat. Garbutt sat at home and accepted regrettably that his career as the *Mister* of Genoa had finally come to the end of the road. He looked back over the years to 1912 and to his three spells in charge. He thought of the many great players he had coached and of the three championships he had helped Genoa gain, all with a sense of enormous pride. He had done all he could and above all else wished for the club's supporters to remember his role in these achievements and not as someone who had been at the helm during a period of decline.

The illnesses and privations he had suffered over the past seven or so years had sapped his strength, and with it, his will to fight. In a very emotional meeting, Garbutt informed the club's directors that he was standing down from the post with immediate effect. This was to be the fourth and final time he would walk away from the position as coach of his beloved Genoa Cricket & Football Club. The separation between Garbutt and Genoa was not to be definitive, at least not immediately. Genoa retained the great man's services in a scouting capacity, an appointment that acknowledged that he had an innate ability, built on the experience gained from his forty-odd years involvement in professional football, to recognise a player with the ability required to succeed in the professional game.

There is no doubting that sentiment also played a part in the decision. Despite Genoa's current difficulties, Garbutt continued to be held in high esteem by all at the club. It was no secret that Garbutt was in a precarious financial position, the war having wiped out any savings that he might have had. Aside from football he had no real experience in any other field and was too old to find alternative employment anyway.

The football club would get another opportunity to display their generosity and respect for all that the *Mister* had done for them when Garbutt suffered an accident in September 1948. Stepping from a tram in Genova's Corso Mentana, he slipped and landed awkwardly, breaking his femur. He had been increasingly unsteady on his feet even before the fall and from that moment on, was unable to walk without the aid of walking sticks.

As he was by now out of contract, Genoa had no legal obligation to their former coach. Nevertheless, and in just one more example of the regard in which the man was held, Genoa Cricket & Football Club agreed to pay for all his medical expenses.

On 4 May 1949, Garbutt joined the rest of Italy in listening in shock at news of the Superga disaster. On that fateful day, Torino, the dominant Italian squad for some years, had been returning from playing a friendly against Benfica in Portugal. With bad weather affecting visibility, crew of the Italian Airlines aircraft had been forced to dramatically reduce their altitude in an attempt to navigate their aircraft back to Turin. With visibility down to a mere forty metres in parts, the plane crashed into the basilica on the hill of Superga and all thirty-one on board, including eighteen players, club officials, (among them Torino's English coach Leslie Lievesley) journalists and crew had perished.

With only four games of the season left to play, Torino had been leading the Italian championship at the time of the disaster. Surviving club officials decided that they would honour their fallen heroes by fielding Torino's youth team, the *Primavera*, for these four games. In a show of solidarity, their opponents for the remaining matches, Palermo, Fiorentina, Sampdoria and Genoa, decided that they would also field their youth teams. Torino, in scenes of high emotion, duly won the *scudetto* once again.

The disaster had a massive impact upon the Italian people, both among those who followed the game of *calcio* and those who had never seen a game. The long-term effects on the Italian national team were also far reaching. *Il Grande Torino* had provided up to ten of the national side and one could argue that it would take until the 1970 World Cup in Mexico before the *Azzurri* would fully recover.

Chapter 14
Back to England

With his increasing medical problems and lack of the financial wherewithal to pay for treatment, Garbutt was understandably worried. His sister-in-law, Dorothy, lived in Leamington Spa and after much cajoling and arguing finally persuaded Garbutt that he and Maria should return to England once and for all so as to take advantage of the National Health Service, which had recently been introduced by Clement Attlee's Labour government.

Saying a permanent farewell to Italy was not a decision Garbutt made without a great deal of heartache. Since first taking up the post of coach of Genoa in 1912, Garbutt had lived in England for only one year, and this in the immediate aftermath of the war.

As had always been the case, however, he faced up to the practicalities of his situation, and bade a sad farewell to all that he had known and loved in Italy, and he and Maria returned to the English midlands to live initially as lodgers with Dorothy in her modest Warwickshire home.

Before leaving Genova there would be the opportunity for one final display of generosity by Genoa Football Club. Garbutt's financial hardship was no secret to the club's directors and three of them, Signors Cifarelli, Tosi and Novieri, arranged a friendly game between a team of former Genoa players and an All Star XI, all the players providing their services for free as a tribute to the *Mister*.

The match was played a week after the final game of the 1950–51 season, on 24 June 1951. Perhaps in fitting with the occasion, honours were even at the end of ninety minutes with the game ending one goal apiece. Seven thousand loyal Genoa supporters attended the game, the proceeds from the gate going some way to improve Garbutt's finances.

Garbutt arrived back on English shores to no fanfare. In contrast to Genova, where he was unable to walk down the street without being accosted by total strangers or asked for his opinion on the latest *calcio* news, Garbutt was left alone. Men did not seek out his hand to shake and talk about some distant memory of a Genoa match or player they had witnessed. Garbutt was anonymous and his exploits were utterly unknown in his own country.

His isolation from the football team, city and country he loved was compounded by the total lack of coverage given to Italian football in English newspapers at that time.

He found it impossible to keep abreast of results, let alone more in-depth news, other than from the occasional letter he received from an erstwhile colleague at the club.

Maria Concetta Ciletti returned to England with Garbutt. She was now twenty-nine (the age Garbutt had been when he set foot on Italian soil as coach of Genoa for the first time back in 1912) and continued faithfully to provide her 'father' with all the care she could give. After taking British citizenship in 1957, Maria finally entered hospital to undergo the operation to repair her hearing which had been so severely damaged as a result of the wartime bombing of Imola.

One matter had been nagging away at Garbutt for a long time now. Ever since Anna had been laid to rest in the Cimiterio Piratello in Imola under a false name, William had made a promise to his wife that he would rectify the situation. With the assistance of friends in Italy, Garbutt and Maria arranged for Anna's remains to be buried under her own name of Anna Stewart (it is the Italian tradition to use a woman's maiden name and not that of her husband in these circumstances). Once this mission was accomplished, Garbutt felt content that he had been able to fulfill his promise to his wife.

In 1960, Garbutt and Maria left Dorothy's home in Leamington Spa and moved the short distance to nearby Warwick, taking up residence in a small terraced home on Priory Road. The passing weeks and months saw Garbutt growing increasingly frail.

Maria continued to care for the elderly man but his needs were now beyond what she could provide and the doctor became an increasingly frequent visitor to the house where Garbutt was by now virtually bedridden.

Although the winter of 1963–64 was not as harsh as it had been the previous year when blizzards piled snow high in the streets, the temperatures were still low and the cold penetrated deep into Garbutt's bones no matter how much coal was heaped on the fire. Maria watched sadly as all life appeared to be ebbing away from the man she had first met as a little girl in Bagnoli Irpino. In his moments of clarity, the two of them would often reminisce about the good times they had enjoyed in Italy, of the great players, coaches, matches and teams. Neither of them was ever fully able to escape their sadness over Anna's death, however.

In February of 1964, Garbutt's condition deteriorated rapidly. On the 16th, Maria was caring for him as she always did, feeding him and doing her best to make him as comfortable as possible. Concerned that his breathing was even more laboured than usual, Maria reassured him that she would be gone only a moment and rushed next door to ask the neighbour to come back with her. After calling for the doctor, the two women walked into the dimly lit room where Garbutt lay propped up against the pillows and sat either side of the bed and each held one the old man's hands. Both fought back tears as Garbutt struggled to make himself understood. Before long, and after telling Maria that she was a 'good girl' he took his last breath and passed away. The primary cause of Garbutt's death was recorded as chronic lymphatic leukemia with diabetes mellitus, a gastric ulcer and polyarthritis as complicating factors. What few items he possessed were left to Maria.

On a bitterly cold February morning, William Garbutt made his final journey the few short miles north from his Warwick home to Canley Cemetery in Coventry. There were no crowds lining the route taken by the hearse; only Maria, son Stuart and daughter-in-law Ivy, niece Joan and sister-in-law Dorothy attended the funeral service. Garbutt's ashes were scattered close to a rose bed called 'Lovers Meeting'.

Obituaries

No obituaries were printed in the English newspapers. The Football Association was most likely unaware that he had returned to England some thirteen years previously, let alone that he had now died.

The situation was very different in Italy. Obituaries appeared in the main sports newspapers and former players and associates of the coach all paid glowing tributes. One of the most illustrious of Garbutt's former players, Napoli's Attila Sallustro, under the headline '*A fabulous Mister*', wrote the following moving article in a Neapolitan newspaper:

The news of the death of Mister Garbutt hurts me to the deepest part of my heart, to that place where men keep their most beautiful memories. Willy Garbutt arrived in Napoli when I was twenty-one years old and had the joy to represent the national university team. He was more than a father to me during the time he was in our city.

He arrived on the training field, accompanied by President Giorgio Ascarelli. We players had known for some time that the fabulous Mister was due to arrive. The likeable man with the white hair and pipe between his teeth had arrived!

Ascarelli said, 'This is Mister Garbutt boys, your new coach,' and then he left with the Mister. Despite us all being initially shy in his company, he quickly relaxed us and made us comfortable. Our training sessions followed the same pattern, ten or fifteen laps of the field, then discussing set plays and so on. He was a typical Englishman, very phlegmatic. I believe Napoli has never had a coach with such a likeable personality. He was a coach of the highest order, the first to arrive at training in the morning and the last to leave, he never moved far from his bench, not even in the most heated of games.

He always told us at the end of the game if we had done well or made mistakes. He never reproached us. White hair, pipe between the teeth, in love with Napoli and Naples, the true style of football, of technique and speed, three passes to the goal! Goodbye Mister Garbutt, from my cold heart.

Attila Sallustro, Naples February 1964.

Older fans of Genoa (and *calcio* in general) read with sadness of Garbutt's passing in the Genovese press. *Il Nuovo Cittadino* reported on the death:

… sad news from England, where, at 82 years of age, the one known as the 'Mister' and who played such a significant part in the story of Genoa. The news of his death on 16 February has aroused deep grief.[55]

Il Secolo XIX reported:

Sad news was received late yesterday evening by the Secretary of the Genoa Club. A letter received from Warwick in England gave news of the passing of William Garbutt, the greatest ever coach of the rossoblu. Garbutt was 82 years of age and had for some time been suffering from an incurable disease. In Genoa's sporting circles, news of Garbutt's death will be met with great regret. From 1912 to 1946, on three occasions, Garbutt led Genoa with great, unforgettable ability. He arrived in the shadow of the Lantern (referring to Genova's famous lighthouse) *during 1912. Genoa had won her sixth title in 1904, but after being a finalist in 1906 and 1909, the team suffered a crisis and in the following two years failed to even qualify for the finals. During this period, the team from Piazza di Ferrari did not even have qualified trainer, team affairs being decided by a committee alternating between Marengo, Franco Rossi, Hug, Pasteur, Storace and Spensley.*

The directors finally made the decision to appoint a 'true' manager, the choice being Garbutt, on the recommendation of the brother of Thomas Coggins, the coach of Genoa's youth team. Garbutt himself was only young, having only abandoned his playing career a short time before following a serious knee injury.

Garbutt set about his task with enthusiasm and got his side to the finals two years in succession. In 1915 Genoa regained her crown but Garbutt

*left to fight in the war. He returned to resume his
leadership of the side, bringing yet more successes.
The last conflict again forced the English coach to
leave Italy. Again he was recalled by Genoa and
accepted the invitation to carry on with the task
that had been interrupted. This he undertook with
his usual enthusiasm and competence.*

*Garbutt was a great diplomat. He knew how to get
the maximum from his players with the minimum
of words and how to prepare them for their athletic
duties in the perfect way.*[56]

Genova's socialist daily *Il Nuovo Lavoro* informed
its readers:

Luigin Burlando (player and coach of Genoa who
had become Garbutt's friend) *has received news
that on 16 February last, of the death in Warwick
of the unforgettable Mister, Willy Garbutt. The
news quickly caused a commotion amongst the
sportsmen of Genova, who will all recall the era
in which Genoa rode the crest of a wave thanks
to William Garbutt's intelligent leadership. The
old sportsmen of this period will not forget Mister
Garbutt; rather they will have memories that
can be reached by a small leap, memories of an
unforgettable past.*

*Our wishes to him come directly from our indelible
memories. And remaining in all our thoughts, for
those qualities of his, of his honesty, attachment,
and above all else, of loyalty.*[57]

Yet another tribute to Garbutt appeared in *Il Corriere Mercantile*:

Mister Garbutt has passed to a better life. With him has passed one of the first true teachers of the game of football; above all else he was a true sportsman, whose honesty served as a role model to so many professionals in the world of the round ball game. Garbutt has died in Warwick, having just turned 81 years old. He passed away on 16 February last, but the news was only received yesterday, and by an old pupil of his, Luigin Burlando, who passed the news on to a sad Genoa Football Club, where the news produced a deep and sincere grief because Garbutt always remained in the mind of the club.

Garbutt has now left this valley of tears, but we are certain that he takes with him the memories of his glorious old team; which had become more a sincere friendship than a profession to him. 'Mister Garbutt': exactly, because this was his true name and Mister Garbutt he remained to everyone. Mister became a kind of qualification, like a 'Doctor of Soccer Sciences'.

Garbutt came amongst us in 1912. Though a formidable right winger, he came to teach rather than to play, thus beginning a long career as Trainer. He stayed with Genoa, other than for an interruption for the First World War, throughout Genoa's golden era. Then on to Naples, to the foot of the Vesuvius, where his qualities as an able technician and gentleman again had the opportunity to emerge. Then to Milan and back to

Genoa in 1937. At the end of his career he suffered a serious accident from which he was never able to recover.

And now to his final 'transfer,' a silent one, appropriate for an honest sportsman like he was, to abandon his uncomfortable armchair for the eternal rest. When Genoa holds its seventieth anniversary celebrations this year, Garbutt will not be the guest of honour as intended by the organizing committee. But those that will be there will be able to celebrate the glories of old Genoa.[58]

Footnotes

1 Garrett, Reid, Schurer & Szreter: *Changing Family Size in England and Wales: Place Class and Demography 1891–1911,* p1 'Among those married women born between 1851 and 1855, over one-third experienced at least seven live births.'

2 B.R. Mitchell: *British Historical Statistics* p58 Table showing that for every 1,000 live births in 1883 in England and Wales there were 137 deaths of infants under the age of one year.

3 F. Scott: *The Conditions and Occupations of the People of Manchester and Salford*

4 F. Engels: *The Condition of the Working Class in England* p52

5 *Athletic News* 14 August 1905

6 *Athletic News* 18 December 1905

7 *Northern Daily Telegraph* 23 March 1909

8 *Northern Daily Telegraph* 25 October 1909

9 *Northern Daily Telegraph* 28 February 1910

10 *Athletic News* 23 January 1911

11 *Athletic News* 18 September 1911

12 P. Lanfranchi: 'Mister Garbutt: The First European Manager' *The Sports Historian* (May 2002) pp44-59

13 D. Russell *Football and the English* p46

14 P. Lanfranchi: 'Mister Garbutt: The First European Manager' *The Sports Historian*

15 A. Ghirelli: *Storia del Calcio in Italia* pp260-261

16 Brian Glanville: *Soccer round the Globe* p59

17 R. Cox, D. Russell & W. Vamplew: *Encyclopaedia of British Football* p43

18 G. Procacci: *History of the Italian People* p396

19 G. Brera: *Storia Critica del Calcio Italiano* p55

20 Lt. Col. F.E. Whitton: *History of the 40th Division* p8

21 R. Westlake: *Kitchener's Army*

22 R. Westlake: *Kitchener's Army*

23 Lt. Col. F.E. Whitton: *History of the 40th Division* p28

24 ibid. p29
25 ibid. p42
26 ibid. p44
27 ibid. p
28 Lt. Col. H.W. Wiebkin, MC: *A Short History of the 39th (Deptford) Divisional Artillery 1915-1918* p33
29 *London Gazette*, issue 31437, 4 July 1919
30 G. Procacci: *History of the Italian People* p404
31 D. Mack Smith: *Mussolini* p41
32 *Athletic News* 8 December 1919
33 P. Lanfranchi: 'Mister Garbutt: The First European Manager' *The Sports Historian*, p51
34 D. Mack Smith: *Mussolini* p88
35 G. Procacci: *History of the Italian People* p422
36 S. Whitaker: *Individual-State-Nation: Anarchist-Individualism and the Origins of Italian Fascism*
37 J. Foot: *Calcio, A History of Italian Football* p39
38 A. Garibotti: *Genoa, dietro la facciata*
39 J. Joll: *Europe since 1870, An International History* p359
40 *Time* 29 May 1939
41 G. Brera: *Storia Critica del Calcio Italiano* p169
42 A. Ghirelli: *Storia del Calcio in Italia* p139
43 P. & L. Gillman: *Collar The Lot* p153
44 S. Zuccotti: *The Italians and the Holocaust* p163 and *Time* 8 April 2002
45 S. Zuccotti: *The Italians and the Holocaust* p54
46 D. Mack Smith: *Mussolini* p304
47 S. Zuccotti: *The Italians and the Holocaust* p55
48 D. Mack Smith: *Mussolini* p347
49 J. Holland: *Italy's Sorrow* p59
50 G. Procacci: *History of the Italian People* p448
51 www.461st.org/
52 Kit C. Carter/Robert Mueller: *US Army Air Forces in World War II Combat Chronology 1941–1945*
53 J. Holland: *Italy's Sorrow* p207
54 W. Robson: *Letters from a Soldier* p138
55 *Il Nuovo Cittadino Genova* 25 February 1964
56 *Il Secolo XIX Genova* 25 February 1964
57 *Il Nuovo Lavoro Genova* 25 February 1964
58 *Il Corriere Mercantile Genova* 25 February 1964

Bibliography and references

Gianni Brera: *Storia Critica del calcio Italiano*, Bompiani (1975)

Antonio Ghirelli: *Storia del Calcio in Italia*, Einaudi (1967)

Simon Martin: *Football and Fascism – The National Game Under Mussolini*, BERG (2004)

Mike Jackman: *Blackburn Rovers A Complete Record 1875–1990*, Breedon Books (2006)

Mike Jackman: *The Essential History of Blackburn Rovers*, Headline (2001)

John Foot: *Calcio, A History of Italian Football*, Fourth Estate (2006)

Alex Graham: *Football in Italy, A Statistical Record 1898–2005*, Soccer Books Ltd (2005)

Mark Robson: *Italy: Liberalism and Fascism 1870–1945*, Hodder & Stoughton (1992)

Giuliano Procacci: *History of the Italian People*, Penguin (1970)

Biagio Angrisani: *Mister William Thomas Garbutt*, La Campanella (2004)

Phil Ball: *Morbo, The Story of Spanish Football*, WSC Books (2001)

Duncan Shaw: 'The Politics of futbol, Spanish football under Franco', *History Today* 1985/35 pp38-42

Scott Grant & Colin White: *Arsenal: History and Full Record 1886–1988*, Lingfield Sport Publications (1988)

Phil Soar & Martin Tyler: *The Official Illustrated History of Arsenal*, Hamlyn (2008)

Giuseppe Fiori: *Antonio Gramsci, Life of a Revolutionary*, NLB (1970)

F. Engels: *The Condition of the Working Class in England*, Penguin (1987)

F. Scott: *The Conditions & Occupations of the People of Manchester and Salford*, (Manchester Statistical Society, 1888)

J.Hicks & G.Allen: *A Century of Change, Trends in UK Statistics since 1900*, House of Commons library (21 December 1999).

S. Whitaker: *Individual-State-Nation: Anarchist-Individualism and the Origins of Italian Fascism*, Leandro Arpinati et al, (1995)

R.J.B. Bosworth: *Everyday Mussolinism: Friends, Family, Locality and Violence in Fascist Italy*, Cambridge University Press (2005)

Denis Mack Smith: *Mussolini*, Granada (1983)

G. Pacileo: *SSC Napoli, Una squadra e la sua citta,*

P. Lanfranchi: 'Mister, Garbutt: The First European Manager', *The Sports Historian*, May 2002.

Dave Russell: *Football and the English: A Social History of Association Football*, 1863–1995, Carnegie Publishing (1997)

Garrett, Reid, Schurer & Szreter: *Changing Family Size in England and Wales: Place, Class and Demography, 1891–1911*, Cambridge University Press (2001)

B.R. Mitchell: *British Historical Statistics*, Cambridge University Press (1988)

Lt. Col. H.W. Wiebkin, MC: *A Short History of the 39th (Deptford) Divisional Artillery 1915–1918*, Naval & Military Press (2005)

Walter Robson: *Letters from a Soldier*, Faber and Faber (1960)

Ray Westlake: *Kitchener's Army*, Spellmount (2003)

R. Cox, D. Russell, W. Vamplew, *Encyclopedia of British Football*, Routledge (2003)

M. Arthur, *Forgotten Voices of the Great War*, Ebury Press (2002)

Lt. Col. F.E Whitton, *History of the 40th Division*, Gale & Polden (1926)

P. Lanfranchi, M. Taylor, *Moving with the ball – the migration of professional footballers*, BERG (2001)

Amedeo Garibotti, *Genoa, dietro la facciata*, Gidielle Edit Genova (1983)

James Joll, *Europe since 1870, An International History*, Penguin (1973)

Matteo Marani, *Dallo scudetto ad Auschwitz*, Aliberti (2007)

Dr Salim Diamand, *Dottore! Internment in Italy 1940–1945*, Mosaic Press (1987)

Eric Lamet, *A Gift from the Enemy*, Syracuse University Press (2007)

Eugenio Corti, *The Last Soldiers of the King, Wartime Italy 1943–1945*, University of Missouri Press (2003)

Peter & Leni Gillman, *Collar The Lot! How Britain Interned and Expelled Its Wartime Refugees*, Quartet Books Ltd (1980)

Susan Zuccotti, *The Italians and the Holocaust*, University of Nebraska Press (1996)

James Holland, *Italy's Sorrow, A Year of War 1944–45*, Harper Press (2008)

Kit C. Carter/Robert Mueller, *US Army Air Forces in World War II Combat Chronology 1941–1945*, DIANE Publishing (1975)

Brian Glanville, *Soccer round the Globe*, Abelard-Schuman (1959)

Index

Other football books from SportsBooks

Charlie Hurley: "The Greatest Centre Half the World has ever seen"
Mark Metcalf

Charlie Hurley was not only a great player, he was one of the characters who illuminated football in the 1950s and '60s. His story will attract great coverage in the papers as he tells of clashes with another footballing great, Jim Baxter, his disputes with the board at Reading when he became a manager and the uncompromising attitude of players and managers during his playing days. Born in Cork, but raised in Essex from the age of seven months, Charlie started his playing career with Millwall before joining Sunderland in 1957. He was to make 400 appearances before leaving for Bolton Wanderers in 1969.

9781899807 69 7
Price £17.99
Hardback

The World at their Feet: Northern Ireland in Sweden
Ronnie Hanna

The story of Northern Ireland's first trip to the World Cup finals when, despite being the smallest country, they reached the quarter-finals. Ronnie Hanna also wrote *Six Glorious Years: Following Northern Ireland 1980–86*

9781899807 74 1
Price £7.99
Paperback

Memories of George Best
Chris Hilton & Ian Cole

Malcolm Brodie, of the *Belfast Telegraph* who covered George Best throughout his brilliant and ill-starred career, called this "the best Best book ever". The authors talked to many of the Manchester United star's contemporaries to find out the true story of the wayward genius.

9781899807 57 4
Price £14.99
Paperback

From Sheffield with Love
Brendan Murphy
Published to celebrate the 150th anniversary of Sheffield FC, the world's oldest football club. The book charts the rise of organised football in Sheffield and Nottingham, the two oldest centres of the game.

9781899807 56 7
Price £8.99
Paperback

The Irish Uprising
Andy Dawson
The story of Roy Keane's dramatic first season at Sunderland, which ended with promotion to the Premier League.

9781899807 60 4
Price £10.99
Paperback

Wembley
Glen Isherwood
Everything you need to know about the 'old' Wembley. Every match ever played at the world's most iconic football venue is detailed here as well as appearances, scorers etc.

1899807 42 X
Price £14.99
Paperback

Accrington Stanley: the club that wouldn't die
Phil Whalley
Fan and writer Phil Whalley charts the comeback of Accrington Stanley the club which resigned from the Football League in the early

'60s. After going bust they re-formed in 1968 and began an astonishing climb back to the League.

1899807 47 0
Price £16.99
Hardback

Harry Potts: Margaret's Story
Margaret Potts and Dave Thomas
Harry Potts was a manager on a par with legends like Matt Busby, Bill Shankly and Bill Nicholson. He brought unprecedented success to small-town Burnley, under the chairmanship of the notorious Bob Lord. This is his story written from his wife's point of view. It's a love story as well as a football book.

1899807 41 1
Price £17.99
Hardback

Raich Carter: the biography
Frank Garrick
The definitive biography of one of the greatest players to pull on a Sunderland shirt. The great inside right had his career ruined by the Second World War but he was the only player to win FA Cup medals before and after it. He also starred when Sunderland won their last League title in 1935–36.

1899807 18 7
Price £16.99
Hardback

Ha'way/Howay the Lads
Alan Candlish
The rivalry between Newcastle and Sunderland is legendary. This book give a report of every first team game.

1899807 39 X
Price £14.99
Paperback

Europe United: a history of the European Cup/Champions League
Andrew Godsell
The story of the European Cup on its 50th birthday.

1899807 30 6
Price £17.99
Hardback

Growing up with Subbuteo: my Dad invented the world's greatest football game
Mark Adolph
The author writes about the colourful life of his father, who invented Subbuteo and turned it into a world-wide success.

1899807 40 3
Price £7.99
Paperback

Fitba Gallimaufry
Adam Scott
All you need to know about Scottish football and a lot you don't!

1899807 45 4
Price £9.99
Hardback

Ode to Jol: A Spurs fan's diary
Alasdair Gold
A very funny look at what turned out to be Martin Jol's last season at White Hart Lane.

1899807 43 8
Price £12.99
Paperback